29.00

ASHE Higher Education Report: Volume 36, Number 1
Kelly Ward, Lisa E. Wolf-Wendel, Series Editors

Cultural Capital: The Promises and Pitfalls in Educational Research

Rachelle Winkle-Wagner

Cultural Capital: The Promises and Pitfalls in Educational Research
Rachelle Winkle-Wagner
ASHE Higher Education Report: Volume 36, Number 1
Kelly Ward, Lisa E. Wolf-Wendel, Series Editors

ISSN 1551-6970   electronic ISSN 1554-6306   ISBN 978-0-4708-8733-2

The ASHE Higher Education Report is part of the Jossey-Bass Higher and Adult Education Series and is published six times a year by Wiley Subscription Services, Inc., A Wiley Company, at Jossey-Bass, 989 Market Street, San Francisco, California 94103-1741.

For subscription information, see the Back Issue/Subscription Order Form in the back of this volume.

CALL FOR PROPOSALS: Prospective authors are strongly encouraged to contact Kelly Ward (kaward@wsu.edu) or Lisa Wolf-Wendel (lwolf@ku.edu). See "About the ASHE Higher Education Report Series" in the back of this volume.

Visit the Jossey-Bass Web site at **www.josseybass.com.**

Printed in the United States of America on acid-free recycled paper.

The ASHE Higher Education Report is indexed in CIJE: Current Index to Journals in Education (ERIC), Current Abstracts (EBSCO), Education Index/Abstracts (H.W. Wilson), ERIC Database (Education Resources Information Center), Higher Education Abstracts (Claremont Graduate University), IBR & IBZ: International Bibliographies of Periodical Literature (K.G. Saur), and Resources in Education (ERIC).

Advisory Board

Contents

Executive Summary

Since its genesis, the concept of cultural capital has permeated educational research. Cultural capital, developed through the theoretical and empirical work of sociologist Pierre Bourdieu (1979a/1984), extends beyond an understanding of financial inequalities to explain the way that privilege and power are perpetuated. Cultural capital is associated with the class-based socialization of culturally relevant skills, abilities, tastes, preferences, or norms that act as a form of currency in the social realm. Cultural capital can act as a form of "goods" in educational settings like schools and universities, offering privileges to some students over others. Culturally based resources can include such things as cultural awareness, knowledge about educational institutions, educational credentials, and aesthetic preferences to which those in an educational setting might best relate.

In educational research, cultural capital has been used as both a theoretical framework and an analytical tool to study such issues as the influence of parental involvement or investments in education on students' educational success; the effects of cultural knowledge, skills, abilities, or competencies on grade point average or achievement; the benefits of cultural involvement in educational settings; college choice decision-making processes; access to and success in higher education; the college transition process; and college student retention.

The Contributions of This Monograph

Through an interrogation of the origins of cultural capital and the ways that it has been adapted in educational research, this monograph offers:

- A demystification of the definitions of cultural capital so that scholars and practitioners can better understand them.
- An examination of the strengths and limitations of the theoretical and empirical scholarship on cultural capital.
- Suggestions of ways that cultural capital can be expanded or better used as a theoretical concept or topic of study in educational research.
- Implications of cultural capital research for educational practice.

The monograph proceeds with an extensive review of the literature, including an analysis of 105 studies in education that considered cultural capital, level of education, methodology, social setting, an analysis of race and gender, and the country where each study was conducted.

Four Definitions of Cultural Capital

This monograph enumerates and analyzes each of the four definitions of cultural capital that emerged from reviewing the work mentioned above:

- Cultural capital as high-status cultural knowledge or competence;
- Cultural capital as knowledge or competence (and sometimes skills and abilities) of the culture that is valued in a particular social setting;
- "Otherized" cultural capital that applies to those in marginalized or non-dominant groups; and
- Cultural capital as part of Bourdieu's larger theory of social reproduction.

The Promises and Pitfalls of Cultural Capital in Educational Research

Analyzing the literature collectively, I assert that many promises and pitfalls should be considered as scholars and practitioners use cultural capital in their work. Promises include:

- The exploration of less tangible perpetuators of privilege such as cultural norms, preferences, tastes, competencies, skills, or abilities;

- The bridging of the agency-structure gap; and
- The implications for research methodology from Bourdieu's work, including the link between theory and data and between macro- and micro-levels of research.

Yet those who use cultural capital in their work commonly ignore certain pitfalls:

- Limitations in the use of an economic metaphor for the notion of cultural capital;
- The lack of attention to moral boundaries in theorizing about this concept;
- The assumption of homogenous class-based privilege in interpretations of cultural capital that may not apply to a pluralistic context like the United States;
- The centrality of class-based analysis, which may disregard race and gender, even as these categories may play a large role in social reproduction processes;
- An implicit deficiency approach, blaming those who "lack" the cultural capital that is valued in particular settings for their insufficiencies; and
- The lack of consistent definitions and interpretations of cultural capital in the research, potentially resulting in a concept that has lost its meaning.

The Future of Cultural Capital in Educational Research

With these promises and pitfalls in mind, I suggest opportunities for future research and recommend ways that the research findings can be applied to educational practice. In particular, I advise reevaluating the definition of cultural capital that scholars and practitioners use; incorporating research studies into Bourdieu's full theoretical framework; giving more attention to race and gender categories; and contemplating the transferability of cultural capital to different countries. Methodologically, it is imperative that scholars using cultural capital provide a definition of the concept in their work and then offer data and analysis that connect with this definition.

Cultural capital has in many ways transformed the way that educational inequalities have been studied. Within the limitations that should be considered in interpreting and applying Bourdieu's ideas, the monograph concludes by calling for more extensions, advancements, and reconsiderations of cultural capital rather than ceasing to use the concept.

Foreword

Rachelle Winkle-Wagner's monograph, *Cultural Capital: The Promises and Pitfalls in Educational Research,* provides an in-depth description and analysis of a frequently used but often misunderstood theoretical construct—cultural capital. As discussed in the monograph, cultural capital is one of those essential theories that researchers and practitioners frequently use to explain inequities in access to and success in U.S. higher education. This monograph offers a critical look at this theory, helping readers, researchers, and practitioners to contextualize the theory and truly understand its uses and potential misuses. It addresses important questions about what cultural capital is (and is not), the origins of the theory, how it differs from the related concepts of social and economic capital, how it is used in both K–12 and higher education research and contexts, the relationship between cultural capital and race, and the extent to which cultural capital can be "taught" or "given" to someone else. It also addresses the important issue of how the field of education values some forms of capital above others and what it means in terms of expanding access to those historically underserved.

I found this monograph particularly compelling because I teach the concept of cultural capital in several of my graduate-level courses. My students find the topic fascinating and see its many uses in explaining inequitable access to higher education. I am guilty, however, of not always assigning them the original source of the theory—Pierre Bourdieu's work. Instead, as I believe is typical, I assign articles that use the theory in a U.S. context. This monograph shows that I am doing a disservice to my students because, as happens in the game of telephone, the farther the message moves from the original source, the more the meaning gets muted and becomes unclear. It is not that theories should not be adapted and used in new ways. In fact, one contribution of this monograph is that it suggests ways that the theory can be expanded. One of the strengths of this monograph is that it reminds all of us of the importance of reading the original work from which a theory is derived and emphasizes the importance of taking into consideration context and nuance. Secondary sources are not sufficient in fully understanding a theory. This monograph helped me to see this context in a concrete way—and showed me the benefits of assigning original source material and of being a critical consumer of research and theory. I will assign this monograph for my class, along with the original source material about which the author writes.

Although the focus of this monograph is on explaining a theory and its use in research, the monograph is helpful to practitioners as well. Not only researchers, faculty members, and graduate students sometimes fail to critically examine the theories they use; practitioners are also occasionally guilty of it as well. Indeed, the idea of cultural capital has gained much popularity among policymakers and institutional leaders—K–12 as well as higher education—and is often cited as a justification for their actions. As such, although a primary audience for *Cultural Capital* certainly includes educational researchers, faculty, and graduate students, it is also appropriate and relevant for practitioners on campuses and state and national policymakers. This monograph is written for anyone interested in access to and success in higher education. In particular, the contents of this monograph are informative to those who work in enrollment management, admissions, financial aid, student services, diversity programs, and TRIO programs and those who focus on providing access and retention programs to historically underserved populations in higher education.

This monograph is related to other monographs published in the ASHE Higher Education Report Series. It is connected, for example, to the recent monograph written by Amy Bergerson (2009), *College Choice and Access to College,* and is also an excellent companion piece to Marybeth Walpole's monograph (2007), *Economically and Educationally Challenged Students in Higher*

Education. Anyone who found these monographs relevant to their interests and work will find much to learn from the present monograph. I am proud to present this monograph and believe it makes an important contribution to the field.

Lisa E. Wolf-Wendel

Series Editor

Acknowledgments

My foray into the concept of cultural capital began during a conversation about my work with African American undergraduate women. What began as a line of questioning regarding my rationale for *not* using the concept, eventually resulted in this monograph. Thus, I would be remiss here if I did not thank Edward St. John and Deborah Faye Carter for beginning, through that conversation (and without even knowing it), my inquiry into this theoretical project. Years later, I presented a conference paper summarizing my thinking on the topic. I am thankful that Lisa Wolf-Wendel was on the same panel, and I am particularly grateful that she believed enough in my work to encourage me to do this project. Her insights, along with those of two anonymous reviewers, were crucial to this finished product.

Thank you to Helen Moore for her cogent and thorough comments on my theoretical understanding of cultural capital. This feedback was integral to my articulation of Bourdieu's work. I am incredibly lucky to have a brilliant graduate student research assistant, Maria Theresa McKinney, whose ear I often bent as I was formalizing my arguments for this manuscript and who was an invaluable part of this project, creating a database for the literature, formatting tables and figures, and reading far less eloquent drafts of chapters (and ultimately the entire manuscript) during the process. Numerous graduate students, acting as research assistants, were helpful in identifying literature and entering that information into the database for this project. Thank you to Tegra Straight, Anh Le, Sheena Kennedy, and Tasha Billie for helping with what was really the unglamorous work of this project.

I am extremely thankful to have family that supports my work. Thank you to my mom- and dad-in-law, Marilyn and Bill Wagner, for coming to help with my family responsibilities at the end of this project. It is not just your granddaughter who treasured the time you were here. To my sister, Brenda Winkle Wilber, thank you for your never-ending support throughout my writing of this monograph (and always) and for reading and offering helpful comments on the entire manuscript at the end. Thanks to my parents, Bill and Carola Winkle, for reading all of my work and supporting it so thoroughly. I am also grateful to Jenny, Corey, and Taylor Hanson for their support.

Finally, to my most precious forms of capital, Mike and Eleanor, thank you. Thank you to my partner, Mike Wagner, for his support from beginning to end (and not just on this project). Although the balance between being a mother and a scholar is chaotic at best, you help to make this experience empowering, and considerably more fun. To my beloved daughter, Eleanor June Winkle-Wagner, I am grateful in so many ways just for your being the energetic toddler that you are and for the way that your presence opens my eyes to see the world in a whole new way.

Published online in Wiley InterScience
(www.interscience.wiley.com) • DOI: 10.1002/aehe.3601

Foundations of Educational Inequality: Cultural Capital and Social Reproduction

THE PAST THREE DECADES have seen the increased use of the term "cultural capital" in classrooms, research articles, and discussions in education. In a recent section of a doctoral seminar that I was teaching, multiple students talked about "cultural capital" with regard to higher education environments. When I asked these students how to define the term, they looked to their colleagues and offered collectively competing, and even contradictory, definitions of the concept. No one linked the notion of cultural capital to a larger theory of social stratification or reproduction. Some students referred to cultural capital as a type of cultural socialization, others referred to it more in terms of academic credentials, and still others admitted that they used the term to refer to the learning of social norms but that they really did not know what it meant. My anecdotal evidence of a term that may have lost its meaning is corroborated by scholarly work. It is as if cultural capital submits a framework of a house without a foundation or any blueprints about how to proceed in the construction. This monograph is an attempt to buttress a theoretical understanding of the cultural capital construct and its applicability to educational research and practice.

In educational research, cultural capital has increasingly been used as a theoretical foundation and analytical tool to study the manifestation of social inequality in educational processes and outcomes (DiMaggio, 1982; Lareau, 2003; McDonough, 1997; Nora, 2004; Roscigno and Ainsworth-Darnell, 1999; Walpole, 2003). Yet it seems that there may be as many treatments of "cultural capital" as there are people who claim this as a theoretical framework or a substantive topic of their work. Scholars exploring primary and secondary schooling have used cultural capital to investigate such issues as the effect of parental involvement or investments in education on students' educational success (Cheadle, 2008; Lareau, 1987); parental socialization toward high-status culture that is rewarded in schools (Kalmijn and Kraaykamp, 1996; Lareau, 2003); the effects of cultural knowledge, skills, abilities, or competences on grade point averages or achievement (Cheadle, 2008; DiMaggio, 1982; Roscigno and Ainsworth-Darnell, 1999); and cultural participation or involvement in schooling (Dumais, 2002). It appears that researchers studying higher education have both taken cues from and worked in tandem with those highlighting primary and secondary schooling. In higher education research, cultural capital has been used to examine and shed light on such factors as the influence of cultural capital on college choice (Freeman, 1997; Nora, 2004; Pascarella, Pierson, Wolniak, and Terenzini, 2004; Perna, 2000); access to and success in higher education (Cabrera and La Nasa, 2001; Davies and Guppy, 1997; DiMaggio and Mohr, 1985; Horvat, 2001; McDonough, 1997; Steelman and Powell, 1989); the college transition process (Walpole, 2003); and college student retention (Tierney, 1999). This monograph interrogates the origins of this theoretical construct along with the ways that it has been adapted in educational research, the goals of which are to:

Demystify the many definitions and misconceptions of cultural capital so that scholars and practitioners can better understand it;

Examine some of the strengths and limitations of the scholarship and thinking on cultural capital;

Offer suggestions for ways that cultural capital can be expanded or better used as a theoretical concept or topic of study in educational research in the future; and

Contemplate the implications of the cultural capital research for educational practice.

Given the increasing use of cultural capital in educational research, it is important to carefully consider the origins of this idea. In particular, it is necessary to tease out the range of possibilities for using cultural capital along with the limitations of the current theory. That is, if this theoretical idea is not fully

understood in its initial intent, it is possible to *mis*use it, resulting in misin-
terpreted research findings and the absence of nuances in the interpretation
of data. If the limitations of the current applications and interpretations of
cultural capital can be better understood, it may be possible to expand the
notion of cultural capital to make the theory more relevant to other issues such
as race, gender, and identity. Used appropriately, cultural capital holds the
promise of providing an excellent theoretical source for research, particularly
research that centers on topics related to class issues, social stratification, or
attempts to understand the perpetuation of equality more generally. This chapter proceeds with an examination of the genesis of theoretical and empirical
work on cultural capital.

Pierre Bourdieu's Theory of Social Reproduction

French sociologist Pierre Bourdieu was the architect of the concept of cultural
capital (1971/1977, 1979a/1984, 1979b/1987; Bourdieu and Passeron,
1964/1979, 1970/1977). Subsequently, scholars across disciplines have proffered theoretical treatments of cultural capital in an effort to shed light on
applications and potential cracks in the uses of the concept (Horvat, 2001;
Kingston, 2001; Lamont and Lareau, 1988; Musoba and Baez, 2009). Before
broaching the task of uncovering Bourdieu's development of cultural capital
and the adaptations of the construct in educational research, it is important
to remark briefly on the scholar himself and on his approach toward the academic discipline of sociology.

Pierre Bourdieu's Sociology

Pierre Bourdieu (1930–2002) was arguably one of the most prolific and
important sociologists of recent history (Robbins, 1991; Swartz, 1997). He is
commonly classified as a conflict theorist. Conflict theory, born out of Marxist
thought, typically asserts a perpetual class conflict and struggle. Like Karl Marx
and his followers, Bourdieu asserted the importance of the economic structure in perpetuating and maintaining inequality. Similar to the two-class
structure that Marx identified, the bourgeoisie and the proletariat, Bourdieu
was concerned that even with the growth of a *petite bourgeoisie* (middle class),

the dualistic class structure between dominant and dominated persisted in many ways. Bourdieu (1979a/1984) asserted that in the continuation of the perpetual class struggle, class exists only through a struggle for distinction.

Marx indicated that one cannot "transcend the limits of one's own mind," meaning that one's acceptance of one's condition may keep one from moving away from it (Bourdieu, 1979a/1984, p. 244). Bourdieu expanded on this notion, suggesting that the class conditions may be doubly limiting by limiting or expanding material conditions that lead to particular practices that may perpetuate material inequalities (such as parenting and schooling) and by providing a world view or legitimation of one's condition that may further maintain these unequal material conditions. Bourdieu was discontented that the physical, material, and economic conditions did not adequately explain the perpetuation of inequality and the more subtle way in which people's seemingly "normal" behaviors or "choices" helped to maintain the social stratification. He extended the earlier Marxist arguments beyond "economic constraints" (Musoba and Baez, 2009, p. 156). Bourdieu expanded Marx's ideas in the context of modern views of meritocracy, the notion that one's opportunities are predicated on one's abilities or merit. The notion of meritocracy is associated with advanced industrial societies and compulsory education, neither of which was instituted when Marx was writing. This examination of meritocracy allowed Bourdieu to scrutinize the way that economics and schooling intersect in perpetuating unequal social conditions. It seemed to Bourdieu that there was something consistent with the lifestyle of people in different class strata, and he made it his project to study this intangible system of preferences.

Bourdieu was essentially concerned with providing evidence that the agency-structure dichotomy, or the idea that the social structure determines one's life chances with or without one's volition, was a falsehood (Horvat, 2001). In other words, he attempted to highlight the *interaction* of agency and structure, or the way that one may be able to use agency to influence social structures in some instances while being affected, even unconsciously, by the social structure in other instances.[1] He was interested in privilege and the way it was perpetuated and reinforced in society. Bourdieu attempted through his work to tender insight into how inequality is generated and maintained. Bourdieu contemplated the agency-structure interaction in part through his study of symbolic power, or power that is often masked, unrecognized, or posed as a cultural norm in a manner that maintains social stratification. Thus, Bourdieu was concerned with those cultural mores, rules, norms, or symbols that aid in the reproduction of and resistance to social inequality.

Cultural Capital Briefly Defined

Cultural capital, developed by Bourdieu as a partial explanation for the less tangible or less immediately visible inequalities, is related to the class-based socialization of culturally relevant skills, abilities, tastes, preferences, or norms that act as a form of currency in the social realm (Bourdieu, 1979a/1984). Cultural capital can be grasped as those culturally based resources that can act as a form of "capital." Culturally based resources can include such things as cultural awareness, knowledge about educational institutions (schools), educational credentials, and aesthetic preferences (such as taste in music, art, or food) (Swartz, 1997). It also includes skills, abilities, or mannerisms, which are primarily habituated and may not be consciously noticed. The aim of his study of these cultural resources was to demonstrate that one's culture can act as a "power resource" (Swartz, 1997, p. 75) in social settings where one can exchange cultural knowledge, skills, abilities, norms, preferences, or mannerisms for social rewards such as acceptance, recognition, inclusion, or even social mobility. Yet the definition of cultural capital was not simplistic, even at its inception.

As Bourdieu's thinking and empirical work developed, his theory of the reproduction of inequality, of which cultural capital was a part, changed too. In his earlier work in the 1960s, cultural capital could be defined as informal academic standards that also are class attributes of the dominant class, consisting of such factors as informal knowledge about education, linguistic competence, and specific attitudes or personal style (Bourdieu and Passeron, 1964/1979). In the early 1970s, Bourdieu refined his definition of cultural capital as academic standards and class attributes to include linguistic aptitude, previous academic culture, formal knowledge of general cultural, and diplomas (Bourdieu and Passeron, 1970/1977). Then in the late 1970s, Bourdieu altered his definition of cultural capital to an indicator and a basis of class position, including cultural attitudes, preferences, and behavior that are conceptualized as "tastes" used for social selection (Bourdieu, 1979a/1984). Bourdieu distinguished among three types of cultural capital: embodied (one's sense of culture, traditions, norms), objectified (things that one owns), and institutionalized (recognition of particular tastes, norms, or values within institutions such as schools).

Cultural capital is primarily acquired in two ways, according to Bourdieu (1979a/1984): through one's social origin (family) and through education (schooling). Cultural capital that is acquired through social origin helps to explain the intergenerational transference of lifestyle or class privilege. Although cultural capital could be acquired through education, primarily formal education in this case, many interpretations of the theoretical idea suggest that it is more difficult to acquire cultural capital *only* through education. Thus, the cumulative acquisition of cultural capital is implicit: one who acquires high-status cultural capital through family origin and through education will be more privileged in society generally. Additionally, formal schooling often reinforces the cultural capital of family origin. More simply stated, teachers, administrators, and others in a school system may reward, perhaps unconsciously, a student who has acquired cultural capital from her or his family over a student who has not (Bourdieu and Passeron, 1970/1977).

In the end, Bourdieu's research focused primarily on those who already have acquired the valued or legitimated cultural capital within a particular setting. The metaphor of a card game suggests that cultural capital affects the cards that one holds in the game. Some of the cards are simply "dealt" to a person (acquired through one's background and sometimes by education, largely not by choice), and some of the cards are deliberately requested or exchanged (acquired more consciously through education), at least in some games (such as Texas Hold 'Em and Omaha Hold 'Em). Yet only some cards are recognized or valuable in the game in a particular context. Each round of the game determines which cards are ultimately valuable. Namely, in one round of the game, a particular hand might be really valuable (a pair of queens might win the hand), but in the next round, the cards from the last game may not hold as much value (the pair of queens might not be valuable because someone has three queens). Cultural capital would maintain that some people are always given the hands that are necessary for a particular round of the game. Thus, while everyone is playing cards and attempting to get the best hand possible, some have an advantage in that they already have been dealt a better hand for the round in which they are playing. This discussion brings up two additional questions: Who determines the rules of the game, and who gets to decide which game is played? This dilemma is at the heart of cultural capital analysis: it begins to call attention to those who get to decide which game is played, the rules of that game, and the cards that will or will not hold value.

Given this varied and complex definition, cultural capital is predicated on a series of other concepts, particularly on the notion of *field* and *habitus*. It is through the interplay of these concepts that Bourdieu began to assemble his full theory of social reproduction of inequality. The impression of cultural capital, habitus, and field is linked to Bourdieu's descriptions and empirical work on the ideas of taste, social distinctions, and social capital. Many scholars employ only portions of Bourdieu's theoretical scaffolding (such as cultural capital), leading to some distortions or mistreatment of the theoretical constructs (Bourdieu and Wacquant, 1992; Horvat, 2001; Lamont and Lareau, 1988). With this caveat in mind, the remainder of this chapter examines, at least momentarily, Bourdieu's full theoretical structure and the ways in which the concepts link to his larger explanation of the reproduction of inequality.

Field

Cultural capital depends on the idea of "field." The field is the space in which cultural competence, or knowledge of particular tastes, dispositions, or norms, is both produced and given a price. The field determines the properties, internalized as dispositions and objectified as economic or cultural goods, that are valid, active, or pertinent in a given social setting (Bourdieu, 1979a/1984). A field is *not* universal; many fields exist. A field is class based and often takes the objectifiable form of a school or a family. It is only within a particular field that cultural capital holds value, produces an effect, or even exists. Fields "present themselves systematically as structured spaces of positions (or posts) whose properties depend on their position within these spaces and . . . can be analyzed independently of the characteristics of their occupants" (Bourdieu, 1993, p. 72).

Relating the concept of field to the notion of conflict between classes, Bourdieu and Wacquant (1992) note, "A field is simultaneously a space of conflict and competition . . . in which participants vie to establish monopoly over the . . . effective capital within it" (p. 17). Consistent with the perpetual discord between classes or statuses in conflict theories, a field is a "space of conflict or competition" (Horvat, 2001, p. 207), the space where people compete for which practices are valued over others.

It is through the theorizing of field and the conflict inherent in it that Bourdieu underscores the fact that cultural capital is a *social relationship*. Those cultural dispositions, skills, abilities, norms, or preferences that are considered "cultivated" (high-status socioeconomically) in a particular social setting are valid only in relation to a particular field.

Bourdieu's notion of field can perhaps also be compared to a card game; cultural capital would be the cards that one could play in the game. He uses this metaphor and notes, "There are no general laws of fields, those being the necessity of commonly understood stakes of the game and players willing and able to play the game" (Bourdieu, 1993, p. 72). Like a game, each field has its own rules or systems of valuation that determine the conditions of entry or inclusion (for example, educational credentials, particular mannerisms or tastes, economic capital) and the social relations in it (for example, who is valued or recognized, whose voice is valued, whose cultural norms are recognized or rewarded) (Topper, 2001). Continuing with the metaphor of a poker game, the field might be representative of a particular game (for example, Seven Card Stud, Texas Hold 'Em). The rules might differ in each game, which dramatically alters the value of the hand that one is dealt (and whether or not one can exchange cards). Thus, one's cultural capital might be very useful in one field and essentially meaningless in another. Or the field could be a casino. One could not cash in the chips from another casino for credit or money. The chips from another casino are essentially worthless in that particular "field." Likewise, one might not be able to "cash in" one's cultural capital in some settings. In educational settings, this argument implies that although all students may come in with "cultural capital," only certain students will be able to exchange (consciously or not) this cultural capital for something of value (such as recognition of their abilities or grades).

Habitus

Integrally linked to field is the sum total of one's cultural capital, the series of dispositions that one has internalized and that one will employ, referred to by

Bourdieu (1979a/1984) as one's "habitus." This habitus or cumulative collection of dispositions, norms, and tastes "functions at every moment as a *matrix of perceptions, appreciations and actions*" (Bourdieu, 1977, pp. 82–83). Habitus becomes a generative practice, the meaning that is given to one's perceptions. It is the capacity to produce classifiable practices and the capacity to differentiate and appreciate practices and products. Thus, habitus is a "structuring structure" that organizes practices and perceptions of those practices and a "structured structure" that is a division into logical classes based on these dispositions (Bourdieu, 1979a/1984, p. 170).

Important to the notion of habitus is that it ultimately functions below the level of consciousness and language. The socialization toward a particular habitus begins in early childhood (Swartz, 1997) but continues well into adulthood as individuals internalize, perhaps without explicit consciousness of having done so, the "rules" that govern the field of interaction and their place in it. This socialization connects to field in that one's "knowledge and recognition of the immanent laws of the field, the stakes and so on" (Bourdieu, 1993, p. 72) are *manifested* as habitus. One's seemingly benign dispositions are actually integral to the reinforcement and creation of the social stratification and one's location in it. As Horvat (2001) put it, habitus is "the mechanism by which an individual interprets possible actions" (p. 209).

In the game metaphor, if cultural capital offers cards to play and field presents the setting where the game is played (or the game itself), habitus provides the approach that one takes to playing one's hand. It influences one's perceptions of the odds of winning or losing and when one feels it is necessary to fold a hand. If cultural capital deals some cards from the bottom of the deck to some players, then a specific habitus for a specific player may have better or worse odds in the larger game. Or, more potently, if some players are given a different type of card altogether (for example, Tarot cards for playing poker), they may not even be able to really play the same game as their competitors.

Habitus connotes the "objective relationship between objectivities" (Bourdieu, 1979a/1984, p. 101). More plainly put, habitus refers to categories of perception and appreciation in the social realm. Habitus is "embodied class" (p. 437). The "schemes of habitus" are embedded in the most automatic gesture techniques of the body, particular ways of walking, talking, or physical

FIGURE 1
Habitus and Material States

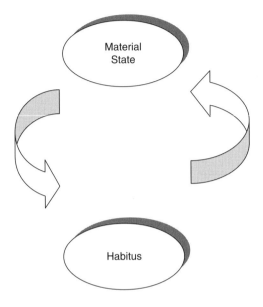

gestures (p. 466). The schemes of habitus act as the primary forms of classification, predominantly below the level of consciousness of language, beyond one's control or will. Through this embodiment of class, habitus engages the fundamental principles of the social world, expressed through the division of labor, the division of work, and the division of domination. That is to say, those in particular class strata display particular physical gestures that connect with their position in the division of labor. Habitus appears "natural" but is actually a complex system of classification and division, a division of bodies and relations between bodies (p. 466). Through this embodiment of class, habitus is integrally linked to material conditions. Although differences in material states (for example, economic conditions) initially lead to differences in habitus, the actions taken because of habitus work to propagate and reinforce stratification between economic positions. Figure 1 demonstrates the perpetual and integral link between the material economic conditions and habitus.

Habitus relates to the cultural capital that one recognizes as available in social settings. One's dispositions, habitus that is used as a form of currency in social relationships, can be rewarded or sanctioned in a particular field. For instance, particular gestures are recognized in a school setting as appropriate, while others are considered distasteful, inappropriate, or awkward. A teacher, perhaps without even realizing it, may "reward" a student who gestures in a particular way by distributing grades, placing students in groups, tracking students in primary or secondary schooling (see, for example, Oakes, 1985), or something that is seemingly benign like simply enjoying a particular student. Yet all these interactions may be an unconscious reward for the student's habitus, demonstrated through his or her cultural capital (demonstrated preferences, tastes, skills, abilities, or norms). Habitus dispositions call about a whole system of conditions that are classified as a "lifestyle" (Bourdieu, 1979a/1984, p. 172). This notion of lifestyle is manifested through the notion of taste, according to Bourdieu. Particular school settings can reward a certain habitus that allows for students to earn greater cultural capital (see, for example, Cookson and Persell, 1985; Horvat, 2001).

Taste

Preferences are manifested through the concept of taste. Tastes are acquired dispositions (that is, one aspect of habitus) to differentiate and appreciate everything from cultural artifacts (art, books, media) to food or clothing to mannerisms, behaviors, or styles of speaking. Bourdieu (1979a/1984) identified three "zones" of taste: legitimate or upper class, which are the least accessible and drive the standard against which all other tastes are measured; middle brow, which primarily belong to the middle class; and popular, which are most accessible and therefore least rewarded in social settings (p. 16). Taste is the propensity and capacity to appropriate a class of classified, classifying objects or practices (p. 173). Taste is the generative formula of lifestyle. Taste can be unconscious or conscious, and it is transmutated into signs, symbols, and value judgments.

Taste transforms classified practices into classifying practices, meaning that as one exhibits a particular taste (employing a classification), one is really making a symbolic expression of class status (turning the classification into something that next works to classify). As Bourdieu (1979a/1984) put it, "Taste classifies, and it classifies the classifier" (p. 6). The demonstration of a particular set of tastes classifies a person into particular social strata. "Art and cultural consumption are predisposed, consciously and deliberately or not, to fulfill a social function of legitimating social differences" (Bourdieu, 1979a/1984, p. 7). By exhibiting particular tastes, one is both "being perceived" as belonging to a particular social status and actually "being" part of that social stratum by manifesting the particular taste (p. 483).

Hence, taste is a "match-maker" (Bourdieu, 1979a/1984, p. 243). Although it may seem accidental that two people of a similar social stratum or class have similar tastes in music, clothing, food, or art, people in a particular class condition may actually be in some ways socialized to acquire and employ that taste. It is the practice of producing and rewarding this taste, the *social relation* of this practice, that explains the way that taste can have a hand in the perpetuation of inequality. Taste is the practical mastery of distributions where one can intuit what is likely to occur in the social realm. It is a social orientation, a sense of one's place. It implies a practical anticipation of social meaning that one can reasonably assume as one exhibits a particular taste, he or she will be rewarded or recognized in a particular way in a social setting.

Like habitus, taste is connected to field. Particular tastes are considered "normal" or emphasized more than others in a field such as a school or family. Habitus is the accumulation of one's tastes as dispositions. Hence, taste, rooted in the field from which one is acting and the habitus or one's set of dispositions, can act as cultural capital, a form of social currency, in the social realm. The social interaction that is the demonstration of taste facilitates social distinctions.

In educational settings, taste can act as a form of social currency but also as a bridge to new knowledge. If a student already knows and values particular referents in a discussion of literature or art, for example, one can benefit more from a lecture or discussion than someone who does not already have those referents. It is one of the ways that taste translates into currency, not only in the social realm but also in the "meritocratic" realm of schooling or college campuses.

Social Capital

The concept of cultural capital is often conflated with the term "social capital" (McNeal, 1999). Bourdieu (1979a/1984) conceived of social capital as "social connections, honorability and respectability" that work as a form of capital in social settings (p. 122). Bourdieu's social capital implies a sense of obligation between people. Like cultural capital, social capital is only relevant in the field in which it is a part. Having particular social connections that can be rewarded as a type of capital in one social setting may or may not ensure that these social connections are rewarded in another setting or field.

Cultural capital could interact and work together with social capital to perpetuate privilege in that one's social capital, one's social connections, drives the availability of cultural capital that one acquires and the cultural capital that is recognized in a particular field. Thus, one's social network becomes a type of "credential" in social settings (Bourdieu, 1979b/1987, p. 249). Habitus (a set of dispositions) and cultural capital (culturally relevant tastes, preferences, skills, and abilities) are rewarded and sanctioned in social settings. Social capital (networks, social obligations, and connections) may help one to locate places (or interactions) in a given field where cultural capital and habitus will be rewarded.

Continuing with Bourdieu's game metaphor, if cultural capital affords one particular cards to play and habitus indicates one's approach to playing the game, social capital specifies where one starts in the game relative to one's social relationships. With an accumulation of social capital, one may get a head start in the game. As a form of capital, cultural capital game cards operate differently when one knows that the casino owner will "comp" some people more chips if they lose (social capital). Or if some people know the dealer (social capital), they could be given inside tips on how to play their cards.

Social Distinctions

One of the primary efforts of Bourdieu's work was to identify the way in which distinctions are made in the social world. These social distinctions are connected with symbolic power, the power that is often "misrecognized as arbitrary" (Bourdieu, 1994, p. 170). Social distinctions then are primarily defined "in and through a given relation between those who exercise power and those who submit to it" (p. 170). In her analysis of Bourdieu's work in light of higher education scholarship, Horvat (2001) provided the example of the increasing number of applications to elite colleges to explain the way that symbolic power might work in the field of education. Symbolic power of this sort appears natural, normal, and correct, and it is widely accepted, particularly by those in the dominated classes (Horvat, 2001).

In his aptly titled landmark book *Distinction: A Social Critique of the Judgment of Taste*, Bourdieu (1979a/1984) presented the results of a survey that was developed after an extended ethnographic and interview study. The survey, taken by 1,217 French people in 1963, aimed to identify cultural dispositions, the consumption of cultural goods, and cultural competence. It measured everything from personal styles of furniture and dress to preferences in food, music, art, theater, and reading material. The *distinction* was a difference in "taste" that Bourdieu defined as "an acquired disposition to differentiate or appreciate . . . to establish and mark differences by a process of distinction" (p. 465). He continued, "It functions as a sort of social orientation, a 'sense of one's place' guiding the occupants of a given place in social space towards the social positions adjusted to their properties, and towards the practices or goods [that] befit the occupants of that position" (p. 465).

Distancing himself from Marx's two-class structure, Bourdieu (1973) claimed that society was structured into three classes or positions: the lower position, including agricultural, tradespeople, and workers; the intermediate position, consisting of heads and employees of industry and intermediate office staff; and the higher position, consisting of higher office staff and professionals. Cultural habits, practices, and preferences, in Bourdieu's thinking (1979a/1984), are linked to one's level of education and only secondarily to one's social origin.[2] Yet only some cultural habits are considered to be "cultured" in society (p. 73). This idea ultimately indicates that "cultural capital" is primarily the possession of the elite in society, those with high class status, which may have been the reason that many adapted cultural capital in this way (for example, DiMaggio, 1982).

Cultural wealth, a way to signify social distinction, is the amassing of cultural capital, or "cultured" habits belonging only to the higher status positions in society; it is accumulated and bequeathed from one generation to the next (Bourdieu, 1979a/1984, p. 73). Although theoretically available to everyone, cultural wealth is only *really* available to those who can appropriate it for themselves. Specifically, only certain people have the "means of appropriation" to be able to decipher particular cultural codes and habits (p. 72). Bourdieu (1979a/1984) used the term "cultural competence" to explain the code by which one can appropriate cultural practices and norms.

Social distinctions are often beyond or beneath consciousness or choice (Bourdieu and Wacquant, 1992). It is through the notion of social distinction, particularly when these distinctions are implicit or tacit, that Bourdieu's discussion of symbolic violence becomes clear. As Horvat (2001) put it, "These unrecognized distinctions perpetuate symbolic violence" (p. 206). Following this argument, people are dominated in and through these social distinctions, but they may not realize it or they may accept it as natural and fair. Thus, "cultural preferences . . . are accepted without recognition of them as an exercise of power but rather are seen as normal cultural expressions that exist within the natural social order" (p. 206).

Symbolic violence relates to the facade of choice in Bourdieu's theoretical apparatus. Those in dominated classes accept their domination in part through what *appear* to be a series of chosen preferences or tastes, physical gestures, or cultural artifacts. For example, one begins to "crave" or "desire" everything from clothing, music, art, or even the food that one's class location would require. This taste and the "choices" associated with it actually work to *maintain* the class stratification. Bourdieu (1979a/1984) explained that often those in classes that require manual labor desire fattier food that would be necessary to fuel their bodies for physical labor, for example. Even if some of the people in this class achieve upward economic mobility and no longer do manual labor, often they will still crave this fattier, cheaper food. Or those in the middle class may develop a "preference" for saving money, acting humbly (not too ostentatious, not too outspoken, for example), or working hard (if one works harder, one can do better in society) so that even if they begin to make more money, their preferences will keep them associated with those in the middle class, simultaneously perpetuating the social order. Bourdieu interpreted this process as "symbolic violence," because class or group preferences appear limiting or because preferences contribute to social exclusions.

Summary: The Social Conditioning Formula and Cultural Capital

Bourdieu outlined a theoretical scaffold of which cultural capital is only one layer in the full structure, suggesting a complex definition for the idea of cultural capital. Pulling together the concepts of cultural capital, habitus, and field, Bourdieu (1979a/1984, p. 101) asserted a social conditioning formula to explain the way that one's lifestyle may be structured. Hence, one's habitus (system of dispositions) times cultural capital (tastes, preference, norms) plus the field in which one is a part (school or family, for example) is equal to the actions or practice that one exhibits in a particular lifestyle (Bourdieu did not include social capital in the social conditioning formula):

$$[(\text{Habitus})(\text{Cultural Capital})] + \text{Field} = \text{Practice}$$

In their review of cultural capital as it applies to higher education, McDonough, Ventresca, and Outcalt (1999) maintained that practice is aimed at securing resources. The acquisition and securing of resources is certainly one aspect of the social conditioning formula, but it is only one piece of the puzzle. Practice, or social action, is the combination of one's set of dispositions (habitus) and one's culturally located preferences, tastes, skills, or abilities in a particular setting (field). The social conditioning formula maintains that practice is fluid and dynamic, an interaction between one's acquired habitus and cultural capital with the social structure, highlighting the interactive process between agency and structure in which Bourdieu took interest. Bourdieu contended that the complexity inherent in this social conditioning formula works to conceal the structure of one's lifestyle and the symbolic space that this lifestyle inhabits in the social realm. Practice is about securing resources, but it is also about classifying lifestyles and being classified into lifestyles that position people in the social structure. It all happens in subtle ways, often below the level of consciousness or apparently so "normal" that it goes unnoticed.

The social conditioning formula suggests that the interaction between agency (individual volition, will, choice) and structure (institution, field, social structure) is not meant to be static, implying that although the structure does at times limit agency because of one's unconscious acceptance of it, Bourdieu's framework still has room for resistance. Figure 2 is one interpretation of the relationship between agency and structure in Bourdieu's theoretical structure. Bourdieu's framework does imply that the structure is at play before one is able to demonstrate agency, represented by the solid arrow between structure and agency. Yet some space for one's agency still exists, perhaps through resistance, to influence the structure in some way. This potential is represented by

FIGURE 2
Interaction between Agency and Structure

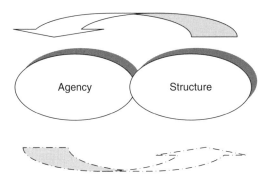

the dashed arrow between agency and structure in Figure 2. At other times, agency and structure intersect, suggested by the overlapping circles in the figure. This intersection or overlap is important to Bourdieu's stance against the dichotomous interpretation of agency and structure. The overlapping circles here imply a bridge between agency and structure. Yet, implied in Bourdieu's work is the idea that one's agency or the actions one sees as available are somehow limited because of and through one's tacit, unconscious acceptance of the existing stratification in the structure. Thus, the intersection of agency and structure in this figure represents both the idea of a bridge between the two and a visual illustration of the limits to one's sense of agency.

Bourdieu (1990) summarized the interplay between agency and structure through his notion of *doxa,* saying "agents never know completely what they are doing and that what they do has more sense than they know" (pp. 68–69). Thus, although agency exists and this agency could in some ways influence structure, the structure may influence agency and individuals in ways that often go unnoticed or are taken for granted. The education system is one location where the agency and structure interaction can be explored.

Cultural Capital and Education

Educational institutions present an excellent location to understand the way that cultural capital is reinforced, rewarded, and acquired. The role of education in Bourdieu's view (1973) is to convert social hierarchies into academic hierarchies, playing a legitimation function to perpetuate the "social order" (p. 83). Although education does facilitate the acquisition of some cultural capital, those students who early acquired the forms of cultural capital valued by the dominant groups will be more highly rewarded. They are also situated in schools or colleges to generate even more of this valued cultural capital.

The school system recognizes particular cultural competencies, which can be expended as cultural capital (Bourdieu, 1979a/1984). Educational institutions then reward those students who are already equipped with the cultural and social capital (through their social origin) that the system presupposes and legitimates (Bourdieu and Passeron, 1970/1977) through the process of making it appear that the reproduction of social hierarchies is based on gifts, merits, or skills (p. 83). Bourdieu (1973) asserted that those cultural habits carried out by families and those practiced by schools work in a "harmonious" way so as to transmit a set of cultural norms, a "cultural heritage" that appears to be the property of the entire society (p. 73). These privileged forms of cultural capital are embedded in the social reproduction process through education: education reinforces symbolic relationships that establish and maintain power distinctions between the classes by reproducing the distribution of cultural capital among different classes (Bourdieu, 1971/1977).

The cultural capital that education implicitly "teaches" to students is closer to the dominant society, according to Bourdieu. For example, pedagogic actions in education may require an initial familiarity with the dominant culture. Yet education does *not* transmit an explicit understanding of dominant culture, nor does it convey an implicit valuing of dominant culture. Thus, Bourdieu (1973) argued, education requires of everyone what it does not give—an understanding of and ability to appropriate dominant culture. It can be measured by Bourdieu's demonstration of statistics indicating that those richest in cultural capital become more and more overrepresented as the level of education increases.

In other words, Bourdieu (1973) asserted that some students have available to them "imperceptible apprenticeships" through their families that ready them for higher levels of education than others. Hence, he claimed, those students with negative predispositions toward schooling will most often result in self-elimination at some point (leaving high school, believing oneself to be a bad student, leaving or not attending college, for example). Bourdieu's claim is that these students anticipate that they will be sanctioned for not possessing the cultural capital that is rewarded by the educational system—the cultural capital of the dominant class—and they react to this anticipated rejection. It follows then that the "laws of the academic market" establish aspirations by determining the extent to which those aspirations can be satisfied by a particular class of people (p. 83). As Bourdieu and Passeron (1970/1977) argued, "The most hidden and most specific function of the educational system consists in hiding its objective function, that is, marking the objective truth of its relationship to the structure of class relations" (p. 208).

Institutions of higher education (and arguably many K–12 schools as well) are ultimately the property of the ruling class. Higher education, Bourdieu (1973) argued, conceals this fact under what Bourdieu called a "cloak of a perfectly democratic method of selection . . . based on talent and merit" (p. 84). Educational attainment is linked to cultural capital as well; one's level of education corresponds with one's available cultural wealth (Bourdieu, 1973). Bourdieu's notion of the educational system as part of the system of reproduction indicates that educational institutions "cannot easily serve egalitarian functions" (Musoba and Baez, 2009, p. 162). Thus, the real success of educational institutions, although often implicit, is in how many students the system sorts out with the effect of establishing and maintaining "distinctions as cultural capital" (p. 163). In Bourdieu's framework, the real success of educational institutions from the perspective of the dominant groups is in how many students the system filters away from it.

It is important to keep in mind here that Bourdieu was most interested in explaining the processes of the French higher education system, which was a "sponsored" system[3] (Turner, 1960), populated by far fewer students proportionately than in the United States. In the United States, the larger, more accessible "contest" system (Turner, 1960) creates more potential strains or fault lines for egalitarian sentiments. For instance, the "cooling out" functions of community college are unnecessary in Bourdieu's higher education system, where people would need "sponsorship" (primarily through their social origin, social networks, and so forth) to gain access to higher education in the first place.

Essentially, what Bourdieu and his colleague, Jean-Claude Passeron (1970/1977), argued is that education plays the role that heredity transmission, the "right of blood" or privilege, played in social orders previously. They asked, "Does [education] not contribute towards persuading each social subject to stay in the place which falls to him *by nature,* to know his place and hold to it?" (p. 210). This view essentially means that education appears to offer credentials based on merit when in reality these credentials may simply be rewards for displaying a particular cultural capital. Education, in this theoretical reasoning, has a direct role in the perpetuation of social stratification, in part through teaching people to accept their place in the social strata and in part through rewarding the cultural capital of those who are already of higher status.

This system of perpetuating, rewarding, and bestowing cultural capital in educational institutions may occur unwittingly to students, teachers, and parents. In the preface to the 1990 printing of *Reproduction in Education, Society and Culture* (1970/1977), Bourdieu concluded that the study "sought to propose a model of the social mediations and processes [that] tend, behind the backs of the agents engaged in the school system—teachers, students and their parents—and often *against their will,* to ensure the transmission of cultural capital across generations and to stamp preexisting differences in inherited cultural capital with a meritocratic seal of academic consecration by virtue of the special symbolic potency of the *title* (credential)" (pp. ix–x). In this way, the school or higher education institution imposes seemingly "legitimate exclusions and inclusions [that] form the basis of the social order" (p. x). Thus, this "huge classificatory machine," as Bourdieu called it, may work despite or amid the best intentions of those in it.

This description of the educational system seems to center more on the *lack* of agency of students, teachers, administrators, or parents, which is one reason that Bourdieu's full theoretical model is necessary to understand a thorough treatment of cultural capital in educational settings. For instance, the concept of field maintains that cultural capital is relevant only in the field in which it is recognized or valued. One could ascertain that agency may stem from engaging in different fields or, in attempting to change the field itself, ultimately altering the types of cultural capital that would be recognized or valued. Bourdieu's point, though, is that reproduction, enacted through education, is an interaction between one's agency and one's structure. Hence, the real agency in his logic may be in this interaction itself.

Promises and Pitfalls of Cultural Capital in Educational Research

It is amid the blueprint of Bourdieu's crafting of and empirical work on cultural capital that I examine the way that this concept has been used in educational research. What follows is a review of the extant research that employed cultural capital as a theoretical construct or a substantive topic of study. The next chapter presents a review of this work with a careful eye toward the definitions and uses of cultural capital. In quantitative terms, I consider the way that cultural capital is operationalized or what variables are used as proxies for cultural capital. On the part of qualitative analysis, I examine how cultural capital is used as an analytic tool or interpretive framework. I also explore the particular methodologies of the studies, the country contexts in which the studies are placed, and the attention that the studies give toward race and gender analysis. "Strikes and Gutters: Examining Applications and Interpretations of Cultural Capital" begins to identify some of the misconceptions, pitfalls, and limitations of cultural capital as it applies to educational research. For example, although an increasing body of work uses this notion, the definition of cultural capital is often unclear or even contradictory, and few scholars use Bourdieu's full theory of reproduction. Yet even in the company of these challenges, this theory still holds promise for scholars and practitioners who desire to use it. The concluding chapter outlines recommendations for future research on cultural capital, with the hope of expanding and strengthening the concept across methodological approaches. Additionally, this closing chapter suggests some implications of the research for educational practice. What follows then is an examination of whether the promises or alternatively the pitfalls of cultural capital have been achieved.

Uses and Abuses of Cultural Capital in Educational Research

PIERRE BOURDIEU'S WORK began in the 1970s and 1980s in France as an attempt to explain the social reproduction of privilege and opportunity, focusing on the cultural skills, knowledge, and abilities that are unequally rewarded in social settings. Scholars in the United States ("American disciples" as sociologist Paul DiMaggio put it) quickly adopted this work, leading to a significant amount of theoretical and empirical scholarship on cultural capital in sociology and in education (Kingston, 2001, p. 88). This chapter provides an overview of the ways that cultural capital has been adapted to educational research in primary, secondary, and postsecondary education.

Methodological Approach and Analysis

This analysis of the extant research on cultural capital in educational research proceeded in two stages. In the first stage, before beginning to collect and analyze the extant literature that employs cultural capital in educational research, I began with a thorough review and study of Pierre Bourdieu's writing and research, the results of which are primarily illustrated in the previous chapter. I collected and analyzed those works by Bourdieu that included either the theoretical development or empirical studies of cultural capital. This research resulted in eleven primary source single- or co-authored books and essays by Bourdieu. Part of this process was reducing Bourdieu's prolific writing to include only those texts that directly developed, described, or empirically evolved cultural capital ideas in some way. Despite earlier readings of many of these works, I spent approximately six months immersed in these texts *before* analyzing the literature that applies Bourdieu's work to educational issues. During this time, I read and reread Bourdieu's work, writing and revising notes to begin to craft an interpretation of the development of his concept of cultural capital.

The second part of my analysis of the treatment of cultural capital in educational research began with collecting articles, books, and essays that either empirically tested cultural capital or theoretically advanced the concept. After an initial broad review of the available studies, I identified three criteria for those studies that would be included in the body of work reviewed in this monograph:

The research must present an *empirical test of cultural capital:* This guideline included those studies that attempted to find variables to serve as proxies for the concept of cultural capital (quantitative studies) in addition to studies that aimed to offer an interpretive analysis of experiences of cultural capital in daily life (qualitative studies); OR

The scholarship must advance a *theoretical treatment of cultural capital:* This criterion incorporated studies that either reviewed cultural capital literature or analyzed Bourdieu's larger theoretical and empirical project; AND

The work must submit an examination of *cultural capital as it relates to education:* This condition incorporated only those studies that included participants who were in educational settings (students, teachers, administrators) or who interacted with those in educational settings (parents, community leaders). Also included were those theoretical treatments that placed the discussion in education or relayed the analysis to educational settings. The scholarship that expounded empirical or theoretical explorations of cultural capital but did not discuss educational processes, outcomes, or issues were not included in this review (for example, an essay on cultural capital and occupational attainment with no mention of education).

The literature was collected primarily through online search engines: J-Stor, Web of Science, Academic Search Premier, ERIC EBSCO, and Google Scholar. I searched using terms such as "cultural capital," "Bourdieu," "education," "schooling," "higher education," "primary education," "secondary

TABLE 1
Literature by Method and Milieu (*n* = 105)

Method	K–12	Higher Education	Other	Total Method
Quantitative	25 (50%)*	19 (36%)*	3 (100%)*	47 (45%)**
Qualitative	17 (34%)	17 (33%)	0	34 (32%)
Mixed Methods	3 (6%)	2 (4%)	0	5 (5%)
Theoretical***	5 (10%)	14 (27%)	0	19 (18%)
Total Milieu (percentage of all studies in pool)	50 (48%)	52 (49%)	3 (3%)	

*The percentages in parentheses in this column represent the percentage of the studies that used that method within the particular milieu (K–12 or higher education).

**The percentages in this column represent the percentage of total studies.

***Includes theoretical pieces, literature reviews, policy briefs, and historical analyses.

education," "social capital," "field," and "habitus." This search, and the subsequent reduction of studies based on my criteria, resulted in 105 articles, books, and essays.

After creating the pool of studies, I analyzed each one for its purpose, level of education, methodology (type of participants, research design and analysis), social setting (schools, families' interactions with schools, communities), whether the study included an analysis of race and gender, and country context. After analyzing the studies relative to their purposes, methodologies, and findings, I began to separate the studies into categories relative to the way in which cultural capital was used (that is, the way that the term was operationalized, defined, or described).

Table 1 presents the literature separated by educational milieu (K–12 and higher education) and by methodology (quantitative, qualitative, mixed, and theoretical). The percentages in the table reflect the percent relative to the studies that employed a particular methodology (quantitative, qualitative, mixed, theoretical). The theoretical studies included literature reviews, historical analyses, policy briefs, and articles aimed at advancing Bourdieu's theoretical edifice. The pool of studies was nearly evenly balanced between K–12 schooling

TABLE 2
U.S. Quantitative Studies by Survey Source (*n* = 32)

Survey	N(%)
National Education Longitudinal Study	10 (31)
CIRP Freshman Survey	3 (9)
Survey of Public Participation in the Arts	3 (9)
Project Talent	2 (6)
Other IES*	3 (9)
Other Longitudinal**	7 (22)
Study-Specific	4 (13)

*Surveys administered by the Institute of Education Sciences, U.S. Department of Education (for example, *High School and Beyond*).
**Panel studies conducted by other organizations (such as *National Longitudinal Study of Youth*).

(48 percent of the studies) and higher education (49 percent of the studies). A few studies discussed education but did not highlight only one level (3 percent). At both levels of education, the plurality of the studies was quantitative (45 percent of the total sample of studies). Of the studies that I reviewed in this monograph, approximately 32 percent were qualitative, 18 percent were theoretical (including literature reviews and theoretical analyses), and 5 percent used mixed methods. The majority of the studies of cultural capital in K–12 education were quantitative (50 percent versus 34 percent qualitative). In higher education, 36 percent of the studies were quantitative, 33 percent were qualitative, 4 percent used mixed methods, and 27 percent were theoretical. The majority of the theoretical essays were centered on higher education issues (74 percent). I aimed to review a balanced number of studies that focused on higher education and K–12 education.

Given that the plurality of the studies was quantitative (45 percent), I delved into the type of data analyzed in these studies (Table 2). Of the forty-seven quantitative studies that I reviewed, thirty-two of them concentrated the analysis in the United States. Of these thirty-two studies, the majority analyzed data that were developed through various branches of the U.S. government (18 of 32 quantitative, U.S. studies, 56 percent). Many of the studies I reviewed here analyzed the National Center for Education Statistics National Education Longitudinal Survey (NELS) (31 percent of the U.S. quantitative studies).

TABLE 3
Literature Incorporating Analysis by Race or Gender and by Milieu (n = 105)

Analysis	K–8	Higher Education	Other
Race	28 (27%)	30 (29%)	0
Gender	12 (11%)	18 (17%)	0
Neither	10 (10%)	7 (7%)	3 (3%)
Total	50 (48%)	52 (50%)	3 (3%)

Next I analyzed the pool of studies proportionate to their analysis of race and gender inequality (Table 3). In relation to the full pool of 105 studies, more than half (55 percent) of the studies included some analysis of racial inequality. Fewer studies provided analysis of gender (29 percent). Only 16 percent ignored or opted not to analyze race or gender.

Finally, I examined the country context of the studies. Figure 3 illustrates a visual representation of the way that the cultural capital idea has spanned the globe. Of the 105 studies reviewed here, seventy-nine (75 percent) were centered on educational issues in the United States. The second largest number of studies placed the analysis in the United Kingdom (ten studies, 9 percent of all the studies), followed by the Netherlands (three studies, 3 percent). The pool of studies includes two studies each from Poland and Russia (comparative studies that included both countries), Canada, Greece, Israel, and South Africa, each accounting for 2 percent of the pool of studies. France, Sweden, and Australia each had one study (1percent each of the pool of studies).

Definitions of Cultural Capital in Educational Research

Categorizing the studies entailed a detailed analysis of the way in which the author(s) explicitly defined or operationalized cultural capital in their studies. That is, many authors imparted an obvious statement as to the definition of cultural capital that they used in their work. Others did not state this definition

FIGURE 3
World Map of Cultural Capital Studies

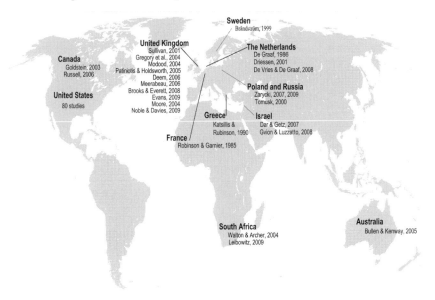

explicitly, but the variables that were chosen as proxies for cultural capital (that is, the way cultural capital was operationalized) or the data in qualitative studies that were used to discuss cultural capital could be inferred to define the term. Some authors offered an explicit definition for cultural capital in addition to providing a discussion as to how the concept was used in the research design. In some instances, some contradictions arose in the way an author defined cultural capital and the way that he or she studied it in the research, more often the case in quantitative studies using large datasets where measures of cultural capital may or may not have been adequate. (This issue is explored in more detail in the next chapter.) From this analysis, four definitional categories emerged: (1) cultural capital as high-status cultural knowledge or competence; (2) cultural capital as knowledge or competence (and sometimes skills and abilities) of that culture, which is valued in a particular social setting; (3) "otherized" cultural capital, which applies to those in marginalized or nondominant groups; and (4) cultural capital as part of Bourdieu's larger theory of social reproduction.

I developed the following set of guidelines for categorization into these definitional groups:

"Highbrow" cultural capital: This scholarship focused on the "highbrow culture" interpretation that has been identified in other reviews (Lareau and Weininger, 2003), considering cultural capital as the property of those in the dominant, high-status, or elite group in society.

"Contextually-Valued" cultural capital: These studies deduced cultural capital to be knowledge or competence of culture that is valued in a particular social setting. This definition of cultural capital links the concept to a larger social system that values or recognizes particular cultural competence, abilities, or skills over others. Thus, all people could have cultural capital, but it may or may not be valued in a particular context. These studies often implicitly related to or casually mentioned (but did not necessarily theoretically treat or define) the concept of field, or the social context in which cultural capital is given its value and meaning.

"Otherized" cultural capital: This scholarship applied or theoretically advanced cultural capital to nondominant, marginalized, or underrepresented populations. Often these studies were critical of earlier work for conceptualizing cultural capital as being accessible only to particular groups.

"Bourdieuian framework" cultural capital: These studies defined or used cultural capital as part of Bourdieu's larger theory, employing what Horvat (2001) referred to as a "Bourdieuian framework" in her examination of cultural capital applications in higher education. This scholarship included concepts such as *habitus, social capital,* and *field.* Research was sorted into this category only if these other concepts entered into substantive analysis or interpretation. If a study casually mentioned other concepts, I categorized the article into another definitional group (for example, the "valued" cultural capital category if field was mentioned but not well defined or treated).

Although each definitional category is explored in more detail with examples from the research in the next section, Exhibit 1 presents each definitional group and a list of the studies that employed that particular definition.

EXHIBIT 1
Cultural Capital Literature by Definition and Education Milieu (*n* = 105)

Definition	Author, Year	K–12	Higher Education	Other	Total
Highbrow Cultural Capital	DiMaggio,1982	•			
	DiMaggio and Mohr, 1985		•		
	Robinson and Garnier, 1985			•	
	Steelman and Powell, 1989		•		
	Katsillis and Rubinson, 1990	•			
	Karen, 1991		•		
	Mohr and DiMaggio, 1995		•		
	Kalmijn and Kraaykamp, 1996	•			
	Peterson and Kern, 1996		•		
	Aschaffenburg and Maas, 1997	•			
	O'Shea, 1998		•		
	Brändström, 1999	•			
	Roscigno and Ainsworth-Darnell, 1999	•			
	De Graaf, De Graaf, and Kraaykamp, 2000	•			
	Lamont, Kaufman, and Moody, 2000	•			
	Tomusk, 2000		•		
	Driessen, 2001	•			
	Sullivan, 2001	•			
	Eitle and Eitle, 2002	•			
	English, 2002	•			
	Tierney, 2002	•			
	Devas, 2004	•			
	Kaufman and Gabler, 2004		•		
	Pascarella, Pierson, Wolniak, and Terenzini, 2004		•		
	Goyette and Mullen, 2006		•		
	Meerabeau, 2006		•		
	Dar and Getz , 2007		•		
	Lundberg, 2007		•		
	Collier and Morgan, 2008		•		
	Gvion and Luzzatto, 2008	•			
	De Vries and De Graaf, 2008			•	
	Noble and Davies, 2009		•		
	Subtotal (percent of all studies)	14	16	2	32 (30)
Contextually-Valued Cultural Capital	Farkas, Grobe, Sheehan, and Shuan, 1990	•			
	Valadez, 1993		•		
	Freeman, 1997	•			

(Continued)

EXHIBIT 1 (*Continued*)

Definition	Author, Year	K–12	Higher Education	Other	Total
	Oakes, Wells, Jones, and Datnow, 1997	•			
	Cabrera and La Nasa, 2001		•		
	Kingston, 2001	•			
	Arnold, 2002	•			
	Bills, 2003		•		
	Farkas, 2003	•			
	Goldstein, 2003	•			
	Astin and Oseguera, 2004		•		
	Gregory, Williams, Baker, and Street, 2004	•			
	Saunders and Serna, 2004		•		
	Walton and Archer, 2004		•		
	Anderson, 2005		•		
	Aries and Seider, 2005		•		
	St. John, 2006		•		
	Martinez-Cosio and Iannacone, 2007	•			
	Zarycki, 2007		•		
	Cheadle, 2008	•			
	Zarycki, 2009		•		
	Subtotal (percent of all studies)	10	11	0	21 (20)
Cultural Capital in a Bourdieuian Framework	Lareau, 1987	•			
	Lamont and Lareau, 1988	•			
	Zweigenhaft, 1993		•		
	McDonough, 1994		•		
	Stanton-Salazar and Dornbusch, 1995	•			
	Smrekar, 1996	•			
	Davies and Guppy, 1997		•		
	Horvat, 1997		•		
	McDonough, 1997		•		
	McDonough, Korn, and Yamasaki, 1997		•		
	Holt, 1998			•	
	Lareau and Horvat, 1999	•			
	Tierney, 1999		•		
	Lareau, 2000	•			
	Olneck, 2000	•			
	Perna, 2000		•		
	Horvat, 2001		•		
	Dumais, 2002	•			
	Lareau and Weininger, 2003	•			

(*Continued*)

EXHIBIT 1 (*Continued*)

Definition	Author, Year	K–12	Higher Education	Other	Total
	Lareau, 2003	•			
	Walpole, 2003		•		
	Weininger and Lareau, 2003	•			
	Modood, 2004		•		
	Nora, 2004		•		
	Monkman, Ronald, and Délimon Théramène, 2005	•			
	Patiniotis and Holdsworth, 2005		•		
	Perna and Titus, 2005		•		
	Walpole, McDonough, Bauer, Gibson, Kanyi, and Toliver, 2005		•		
	Deem, 2006		•		
	Dumais, 2006	•			
	Lee and Bowen, 2006	•			
	Russell, 2006	•			
	Christ and Wang, 2008	•			
	Salisbury, Umbach, Paulsen, and Pascarella, 2009		•		
	Wells, 2008		•		
	Musoba and Baez, 2009		•		
	Evans, 2009	•			
	Martin and Spenner, 2009		•		
	Moore, 2004	•			
	Subtotal (percent of all studies)	18	20	1	39 (37)
Otherized Cultural Capital	Olneck, 2000 (multicultural education cultural capital)	•			
	Franklin, 2002 (collective cultural capital)	•			
	Pradl, 2002 (existing cultural capital)	•			
	Span, 2002 (black cultural capital)	•			
	Carter, 2003 (black cultural capital)	•			
	Nasir and Saxe, 2003 (shifting cultural capital)	•			
	Bullen and Kenway, 2005 (subcultural capital)	•			
	Pearce and Lin, 2005 (nondominant cultural capital)		•		
	Yosso, 2005 (community cultural wealth)		•		
	Pearce and Lin, 2007 (nondominant capital)		•		
	Brooks and Everett, 2008 (youth cultural capital)	•			

(Continued)

EXHIBIT 1 (*Continued*)

Definition	Author, Year	K–12	Higher Education	Other	Total
	Leibowitz, 2009 (Yosso's, 2005, community cultural wealth)		•		
	Núñez, 2009 (intercultural capital)		•		
	Subtotal (percent of all studies)	8	5	0	13 (12)
	Total (percent of all studies)	50 (48)	52 (49)	3 (3)	

I separated the studies in terms of whether they addressed primary or secondary education (K–12) or higher education and listed them in chronological (rather than alphabetical) order to illustrate the way that these definitions have developed. Regarding the definitional groups, the frequency of use was as follows: thirty-two studies (30 percent of the total number of studies) employed a highbrow cultural capital definition; twenty-one studies (20 percent of the pool of literature) used a contextually-valued cultural capital interpretation; thirty-nine studies (37 percent) of the studies used Bourdieu's larger theoretical framework; and thirteen studies (12 percent) considered "otherized" cultural capital. Slightly more studies reflected otherized cultural capital at the K–12 level in this pool of studies. Otherwise in these definitional groups, the number of studies that explored higher education or K–12 education was relatively similar.

Categorizing the work on cultural capital into these definitional groups clarifies in part the trajectory of the way in which researchers in education have interpreted this theoretical notion. DiMaggio's work (1982) on cultural capital launched the notion of cultural capital as the acquisition of highbrow cultural knowledge and competence and this definition would become one of the dominant interpretations of the concept in the 1980s and 1990s. More recent advances (the late 1990s and early 2000s) in cultural capital have started to place this construct in Bourdieu's larger theory of the social reproduction of class inequality: first with a notion of the concept as a scarce resource of cultural competence, knowledge, and skills that are "valued" in a particular social setting; and in concert with other concepts like habitus, field, and social capital. Those studies that considered cultural capital as it applies to those in non-dominant or "otherized" groups are more recent advances on the topic, released in the last decade (since 2000). Sociologists began to use cultural capital in their scholarship in the early 1980s, starting shortly after Bourdieu's development of it. This work primarily focused on education at the primary and secondary levels. Some sociologists did begin to consider cultural capital applications to higher education in the late 1980s and early 1990s. Higher education scholars followed about a decade later, beginning to incorporate cultural capital into their work in the late 1990s, and the use of the concept mushroomed from that point into the new millennium.

Cultural Capital in Educational Research

Cultural capital has been used as a vehicle to explore numerous topics related to inequalities in education. In primary and secondary education, researchers have considered such factors as the influence of cultural capital on parental involvement or investments in education, parental socialization toward high-status culture that is rewarded in schools, and the effects of cultural capital on grade point averages or academic achievement (Cheadle, 2008; DiMaggio, 1982; Kalmijn and Kraaykamp,1996; Lareau, 1987, 2003; Roscigno and Ainsworth-Darnell, 1999).

The field of higher education has taken cues from the field of sociology in using cultural capital as a theoretical framework and a variable for study. In the study of higher education, cultural capital has been used as a theoretical structure and analytical tool to explore the college choice process (Freeman, 1997; Nora, 2004; Pascarella, Pierson, Wolniak, and Terenzini, 2004; Perna, 2000), access to and success in higher education (Cabrera and La Nasa, 2001; Davies and Guppy, 1997; DiMaggio and Mohr, 1985; McDonough, 1997; Steelman and Powell, 1989), the college transition process (Walpole, 2003), and college student retention (Tierney, 1999).

Taking a seamless educational approach in this chapter, including primary school through graduate school, I present the research in terms of the definitional category of which it is a part. This approach offers a representation of the genesis and evolution of cultural capital in educational research and simultaneously demonstrates the way in which one level of education informs and influences the next. Likewise, the research and theory related to one level of education (primary and secondary education) connects with and affects the next level (higher education). Hence, I review the literature in each definitional grouping: highbrow, valued, otherized, and as part of Bourdieu's theory of social reproduction.

Highbrow Cultural Capital

The predominant interpretation of cultural capital, particularly as it relates to primary and secondary education, was initiated with DiMaggio's survey (1982) of eleventh graders' school success (Project Talent). He compared cultural capital (defined as involvement in highbrow cultural activities) with high school grades, asserting that cultural capital does affect academic achievement. DiMaggio (1982) defined cultural capital as the knowledge or competence of dominant or elite culture. His initial study expounded rich measures of involvement in art, music, and literature and markers for academic ability. Using the same operationalization for cultural capital, DiMaggio and Mohr (1985) continued analyzing the Project Talent data, finding significant effects of the respondents' cultural capital (participation in highbrow cultural activities) on college attendance, college completion, and enrollment in graduate education. The measure of family status was simply father's education, potentially a weak variable for family status (Kingston, 2001), a limitation that DiMaggio (1982) recognized. Nonetheless, the subsequent scholarship often used parental education or income level to connote family status in the way that DiMaggio initiated (1982; DiMaggio and Mohr, 1985).

Regardless of its limitations, the operationalization of cultural capital as knowledge or competence of highbrow culture (fine art, classical music, theater, and so on) proffered by DiMaggio and his colleagues (DiMaggio, 1982; DiMaggio and Mohr, 1985; Mohr and DiMaggio, 1995) provides the backdrop on which other scholars have painted a picture of cultural capital in schools (Kingston, 2001; Lareau and Weininger, 2003).

Successive work on cultural capital as it relates to education, particularly scholarship in sociology, has largely employed DiMaggio's (1982) interpretation of the concept as the knowledge or competence of elite, high-status culture (see, for example, Aschaffenburg and Maas, 1997; De Graaf, 1986; Eitle and Eitle, 2002; Kalmijn and Kraaykamp, 1996; Katsillis and Rubinson, 1990; Robinson and Garnier, 1985; Roscigno and Ainsworth-Darnell, 1999; Sullivan,

2001). In the highbrow culture definition of cultural capital, researchers have considered such issues as parental socialization toward high-status culture that is rewarded in schools (Kalmijn and Kraaykamp, 1996); the effects of knowledge or competence of highbrow culture on grade point averages, achievement, or general success (Aschaffenburg and Maas, 1997; English, 2002; Katsillis and Rubinson, 1990; Roscigno and Ainsworth-Darnell, 1999); degree choice in college (Goyette and Mullen, 2006); upward social mobility (Kalmijn and Kraaykamp, 1996); and access to higher education (Karen, 1991; Tierney, 2002).

Picking up where DiMaggio and his colleagues left off, exploring racial differences in the accumulation of cultural capital among parents, Kalmijn and Kraaykamp (1996) analyzed data from the Survey of Public Participation in the Arts. Given that the dataset included no available measurement of family income, cultural capital was operationalized as parental education and rural residence. The findings indicated that Black parental exposure and incorporation to high-status culture has increased more than it has for White students, suggesting that cultural capital may be one route toward upward mobility for racial minority groups. Yet without a variable for background family income, the reference to upward social mobility may be questionable, as Kingston (2001) noted in his theoretical analysis of cultural capital use in research.

Also analyzing data from the Survey of Public Participation in the Arts, Aschaffenburg and Maas (1997) inquired into the relationship between cultural capital and educational careers, including both parental and student cultural capital in one model. Student cultural capital was operationalized as taking classes in highbrow cultural activities (such as painting classes and music classes). Parental cultural capital was measured as those activities that specifically might advance their children's highbrow cultural capital (such as engaging their children in arts activities and taking children to a museum or theater). The findings suggest that the cultural capital of one's parents and cultural participation outside school relate to success in education but that early effects of cultural capital acquisition diminish over time. That is, as a student progresses through school, early cultural capital matters less. This finding underscores the importance of cultural capital acquisition in schooling. The modeling and results in this study may have paved the way for interpretations of cultural capital that were more robust and considerations of the field in which cultural capital was or was not rewarded (the contextually-valued cultural capital interpretation).

Similar to Aschaffenburg and Maas (1997), Roscigno and Ainsworth-Darnell (1999) granted a measure of cultural capital that included involvement in highbrow cultural classes (such as painting, music, and dance) along with family background variables for cultural capital (measured by family income, parental education, and parents' occupation) in their model. The analysis of the NELS dataset indicated that although cultural capital did affect grades and achievement, Black and low socioeconomic students received fewer rewards (measured by grade point average and mathematics-reading composite scores) for cultural capital than did White students. Also connecting cultural capital with racial inequality but taking a different tack, English's theoretical reasoning (2002) examined the achievement gap between White students and students of color (in this case, African American and Latino students) in primary and secondary schooling using a notion of high-status cultural capital where knowledge of dominant class culture, often the possession of White students according to these results, is rewarded in achievement tests.

Similar to educational research at the K–12 level, educational researchers who study higher education have often used a definition of cultural capital that links it to high-status, elite cultural signals. Pascarella, Pierson, Wolniak, and Terenzini (2004) analyzed data from the National Study of Student Learning (NSSL) along with the National Center on Education Statistics Integrated Postsecondary Education Data System (IPEDS) for institutional data, maintaining that cultural capital (defined as knowledge of high-status culture) influenced both the types of institutions that students attended and the experiences that students had once they enrolled. First-generation college students whose parents were not college educated were significantly disadvantaged. Background cultural capital was measured by parental educational attainment like for many other studies, but the student outcome measures were more complex, focusing on openness to diversity, reasoning, critical thinking, and comprehension scores. Additionally, the student cultural capital variables were more full bodied in that they included many of the on-campus activities in which students were engaged. Yet the background cultural capital variable (parent educational attainment) may not serve as a good proxy for even highbrow cultural capital because it does not identify cultural involvement or past experience. These scholars ultimately advocated for helping first-generation college students to acquire the necessary cultural capital to facilitate success in college.

Making a similar argument to Pascarella and his coauthors in a theoretical analysis of the role of the notion of "college student," Collier and Morgan (2008) used a high-status cultural capital interpretation to maintain that one way to achieve greater equality in higher education is to focus on the mastery of this role. In this view, if students could be taught the role of "college student," it would help them to acquire cultural capital.

Yet once students are enrolled in college, the possession of high-status cultural capital is linked to students' choice of academic field, according to the results of Goyette and Mullen's (2006) analysis of the NELS and Baccalaureate and Beyond datasets where low socioeconomic students were more likely to choose vocationally related majors in college. Although the background cultural capital measures were similar to other studies (parental education and income level), this study operationalized cultural capital that students acquire in college as familiarity with highbrow culture, writing skills, and learned knowledge of history, culture, and politics. This interpretation allows for knowledge and competence of highbrow culture alongside skills and abilities that one acquires in education.

The highbrow culture interpretation of cultural capital has numerous limitations. Perhaps the most important is that it is not necessarily consistent with Bourdieu's more nuanced definition of cultural capital, which asserted cultural capital as particular cultural competencies, knowledge, or skills that are rewarded in a certain setting (field). Additionally, the application of this interpretation in research studies divorces the knowledge and competence that one has of highbrow culture from one's abilities to be able to appropriate this knowledge and competence. As Lareau and Weininger (2003) reflected in their review of extant cultural capital studies, this outcome results in research where "the salience of cultural capital is tested by assessing whether measures of 'highbrow' cultural participation predict educational outcomes (such as grades) independently of various 'ability measures' (such as standardized test scores)" (p. 568). Finally, criticisms of this interpretation have grown because it may inadvertently devalue the cultural knowledge, skills, abilities, or competencies of those in marginalized groups such as people of color in the American context (see Carter, 2003; Yosso, 2005).

Another limitation, or perhaps a cautionary note, prevalent in many of the cultural capital interpretations, is the operationalization of background cultural capital in many of the quantitative studies. Overwhelmingly, and perhaps because scholars are constrained by their datasets, background cultural capital is operationalized in some variation of three variables: parental educational attainment, parental income, and parental occupational attainment. Assumptions are made that income, education, and occupation can connote a particular level of access to highbrow cultural resources. For example, in higher education, a student with parents who are college educated, middle to upper income, and employed in high-status occupations will likely have access to many of the dominant highbrow cultural resources. Although it may often be the case that cultural capital is linked to elite culture, without measures of actual experiences (such as cultural involvement in and out of school), this interpretation may simply be an assumption based on class status that may or may not be grounded in lived experience. That is, if a student does not have a close interaction with her or his parents, for instance, parents' attainment of occupation, income, or education may or may not really result in the acquisition of cultural capital for the student.

Contextually-Valued Cultural Capital

Although it may at first seem like splitting hairs, I am arguing here for a clearer distinction between those scholars who can be considered in DiMaggio's (1982) highbrow cultural capital definitional category and those whose work suggests a treatment of this theoretical idea that allows for a more nuanced interpretation of the concept. This interpretation of cultural capital considers it to be the knowledge or competence (and sometimes the skills and abilities) of the culture that is valued in a particular setting (see, for example, Anderson, 2005; Aries and Seider, 2005; Astin and Oseguera, 2004; Goldstein, 2003; Gregory, Williams, Baker, and Street, 2004; Martinez-Cosio and Iannacone, 2007; Oakes, Wells, Jones, and Datnow, 1997; St. John, 2006).

The contextually-valued cultural capital definition shifts away from the high-status culture interpretation to allow for more nuances. It is contextualized and dependent on the setting. With this interpretation, one could possess cultural capital that may or may not be valued in a particular setting. Rather than suggesting that one simply does or does not have cultural capital, the high-status cultural capital definition maintains that cultural capital is the property of the dominant or elite class. The contextually-valued cultural capital interpretation implies that particular knowledge, competence, skills, or abilities "provide access to scarce rewards" (Lareau and Weininger, 2003, p. 587). Lareau largely employed this interpretation in her ethnographic work on family and schools (2000, 2003), although she also placed her work in Bourdieu's larger theory of social reproduction, as I explain below. Although scholars using the contextually-valued cultural capital interpretation do not necessarily place cultural capital in Bourdieu's larger theory of social reproduction (including concepts such as habitus, field, or social capital), the notion of "field" is often implied or assumed in that cultural capital may be of value only in a certain way in a particular setting.

The contextually-valued interpretation of cultural capital has been used to examine such educational issues as informal academic standards (Farkas, 2003); use of linguistic resources (Goldstein, 2003); detracking efforts in primary or secondary schooling (Oakes, Wells, Jones, and Datnow, 1997); inequalities in access to literacy (Gregory, Williams, Baker, and Street, 2004); parental and family involvement in schooling (Cheadle, 2008; Martinez-Cosio and Iannacone, 2007); college choice decision-making processes (Astin and Oseguera, 2004; Freeman, 1997); students' perceptions of financial aid for college (St. John, 2006); and the identity development of college students related to their socioeconomic background (Aries and Seider, 2005).

Farkas (2003) and his colleagues examined the informal academic standards that are subtly or explicitly rewarded in schools (Farkas, Grobe, Sheehan, and Shuan, 1990). Through a study of district-level data of seventh- and eighth-grade students, Farkas and his colleagues (1990) found that teachers' rewarding of students' noncognitive abilities (as measured by informal academic standards such as students' and teachers' background characteristics and teachers' judgment of students' work habits, appearance, and coursework mastery) affected students' cognitive development (indirectly affecting grades). In other words, students' grades were indirectly affected by teachers' implicit judgments of a student's background and ability. Teachers' judgments were not necessarily based on skill or merit but on perceptions of background. The proxy for background cultural capital was a dummy variable for poverty (in poverty, not in poverty). This proxy for cultural capital assumes that one does or does not have cultural capital. Then students' work habits were used as another proxy for cultural capital, taken from a survey administered to teachers. In this study, as in many others, the theoretical model for understanding cultural capital, including the teacher's background, students' background, and students' habits in schooling, was far more complex than what the data allowed for with the actual variables.

Oakes, Wells, Jones, and Datnow (1997) used cultural capital as a theoretical framework for their exploration into detracking efforts in schools. Their longitudinal case study of ten racially and socioeconomically mixed secondary schools interrogated race and class norms and found that perceptions of race and class informed teachers', students', and parents' notions of what constituted "ability." In this way, race and class stereotypes often led teachers, students, and parents to assume some students were high or low ability based on their race or class categories rather than their actual intellectual capabilities. Manifestations of cultural capital (defined as ways of knowing) were interpreted as privileging some ways of knowing over others. But Oakes and her colleagues went one step further, suggesting that cultural capital actually became a marker of ability in schools, which enhanced privilege for White and wealthy students. Another way of explaining it is that teachers' perceptions that a student had the cultural capital that the teacher valued was seen as an indication of students' academic ability.

Cheadle's (2008) hierarchical modeling with the Early Childhood Longitudinal Study data built on Lareau's (2003) work on concerted cultivation (a parenting style that was associated with the cultural capital valued in schooling) at the aggregate level. This study explored cultural capital as parental investments in education in relation to math and reading achievement in primary school. Here, the variables for cultural capital (captured through the term "concerted cultivation") were a composite measure of parenting that included such factors as measures of children's daily lives, use of language, and parental involvement with schools. Findings suggested that parents' investments in culturally relevant education, both in and out of schooling, did mediate socioeconomic and racial disparities in education. This multilevel approach allowed for a simultaneous analysis of students' family backgrounds and their experiences in schooling. The operationalization of cultural capital was also robust in that it included multiple markers of cultural involvement and competences (such as lessons in arts-oriented or sports activities) or parents' ability to appropriate cultural capital (such as attending events and involvement in schools).

Taking a qualitative approach, Valadez (1993) employed ethnographic interviews, observations, and document analysis to ascertain the influence of cultural capital on the aspirations of nontraditional (age 25 and older) community college students. In this case, cultural capital was interpreted as the necessary knowledge or skills for students to understand how to navigate further educational study. This study combined data from faculty, students, and administrators to put forward different interpretations of cultural capital based on the position from which the participant came in the institution. The findings indicated that participants perceived that the cultural capital needed for educational advancement and career mobility was middle class and White. Valadez concluded that this situation led to participants' feeling as though they did not belong in higher education. This factor could be related to attrition or lack of transferring to four-year institutions for some students.

Also examining access to higher education, Freeman (1997) used cultural capital in concert with Coleman's "Social Capital" (1988) to craft the notion of channeling in her qualitative study of the college choice process of African American high school students (comparing those in an inner city school with those in a private high school). Her argument was that channeling connotes the way in which environmental factors, including cultural capital (defined as cultural knowledge or competence that is valued or dominant), influence students' decisions about college attendance and enrollment.

Aries and Seider (2005) knitted together both the high-status interpretation of cultural capital with the contextually-valued cultural capital definition to qualitatively study the identity of lower-income students at an elite and a state college. Their findings suggested that lower-income students experienced more negative influences on their identity in the elite college setting. Although it was an interview-based study, the authors still started with parents' educational level as a marker of background cultural capital in students. The questions asked of participants were very nuanced, however, attempting to uncover the way that participants defined their own cultural capital in relation to the cultural capital that was rewarded on campus. Consequently, the findings focused not just on knowledge and competence but also on skills and abilities associated with the cultural capital that is valued in a particular setting. The addition of skills and abilities begins to explain ways that a student can or cannot actually appropriate his or her acquired cultural capital (that is, exchange cultural capital for educational rewards).

Also considering socioeconomic background related to cultural capital, St. John (2006) argued for a greater emphasis on the role of family income in considerations of cultural capital. Through qualitative data, he demonstrated that students' cultural capital is linked to their perceptions of financial accessibility to college. That is, concerns about finances can shape college decision-making processes (such as whether to enroll and whether to persist). The implications of this study suggest that discussions about cultural capital should also include references to economic capital and the way that finances shape students' accessibility to college-related cultural knowledge and competence. Proxies for cultural capital in research then should include not only parents' educational attainment but also family income levels, according to this study. St. John began to lodge a critique of the common way that cultural capital is operationalized, calling for more nuance and complexity.

At times, cultural capital may relate to inequalities between types of institutions and programs that students attend at particular universities. Some work indicates that cultural capital affects the selectivity of institutions where students will enroll; higher socioeconomic students typically have the cultural capital that leads to more selective institutional enrollment, according to Astin and Oseguera (2004). Cultural capital was rooted in Farkas's work and was framed as the knowledge that a student may or may not have of the rewards of attending an elite postsecondary institution. Although cultural capital was mentioned in the implications and discussion, no explicit variable was applied to the cultural capital concept in the study. But it seems that some assumptions are made about background cultural capital based on parents' education levels.

Examining the college experiences of Latino students, Saunders and Serna (2004) analyzed primarily the qualitative aspects of the NELS dataset, implying that college or access intervention programs may be critical in affording students an opportunity to gain the cultural capital valued in a particular setting through the ability to mobilize personal and institutional support. Although this study suggested a more dynamic interpretation of cultural capital, the analysis merged cultural and social capital at times rather than identifying the variables that relate to each of these concepts individually. It was not always clear exactly what was considered "cultural capital" in the analysis.

Also examining cultural capital relative to the accumulation of privilege, Anderson (2005) penned a theoretical analysis of the way that the valued cultural capital can shift to maintain the privilege of some groups. In the case of his paper, White students who acquire diversity-related cultural capital through higher education diversity courses and other programmatic efforts may begin to shift the "valued" cultural capital on campus to "diversity cultural capital." Thus, White students could gain privileges on campus by simply having acquired "diversity" knowledge and skills.

The contextually-valued cultural capital interpretation offers more nuance in the way that cultural capital is defined and studied in educational research. Rather than a zero-sum game where one either has cultural capital or does not, this interpretation often theoretically suggests that everyone could have cultural capital, although some forms of it may be valued more in a particular setting. This interpretation is more relevant to Bourdieu's theoretical reasoning, as it allows for cultural capital to be contextualized, taking into account, at least implicitly, the notion of field (that is, the setting and context that structures the rules of the game). It is probably no accident that the contextually-valued cultural capital interpretation includes more theoretical analyses that attempt to evolve the way that the cultural capital is applied in educational research (see, for example, Anderson, 2005; Arnold, 2002; Kingston, 2001).

The quantitative studies still at times suffer from the often used parental education, occupation, or income as proxies for background cultural capital (see, for example, Farkas, Grobe, Sheehan, and Shuan, 1990). Moreover, many quantitative studies used a dummy variable for background cultural capital, implying that one either does or does not have it, primarily because of limitations in the datasets. Additionally, many of the datasets do not include richer measurements of cultural participation, skills, or abilities. The examples of multilevel statistical modeling that take a contextually-valued cultural capital interpretation (for example, Cheadle, 2008) allow for a simultaneous study of family, school, and even district-level data. These models submit a richer way to understand the way that one's background experiences relative to cultural capital influence educational experiences.

The contextually-valued cultural capital category contains more qualitative methodologies than the highbrow cultural capital interpretation. These interpretive research designs allow for a reflection of cultural capital that depends on context. Even so, a challenge with many of the qualitative studies is that it is often unclear exactly how cultural capital was used in the analysis of qualitative data.

An additional advancement with the contextually-valued cultural capital interpretation is a clearer addition of the skills and abilities associated with cultural capital. The highbrow cultural capital interpretation focuses primarily on the knowledge or competence of high-status culture, a limitation recognized by Lareau and Weininger (2003) in their theoretical analysis of these studies. The scholars, using a notion of cultural capital associated with that which is rewarded in a particular setting, often include skills and abilities along with knowledge and competence (for example, Aries and Seider, 2005; Valadez, 1993). Yet some have criticized these studies, saying that they continue to underline the dominant forms of cultural capital. Accordingly, the nondominant branch of cultural capital scholarship is growing.

Nondominant or Otherized Cultural Capital
The inclination in recent years has been to make the idea of cultural capital more applicable to marginalized, often "otherized" populations (for example, Carter, 2003; Nasir and Saxe, 2003; Olneck, 2000; Yosso, 2005). In this spirit, scholars have identified more communal definitions of cultural capital that shift away from the assumption of an individualized, personal possession of

cultural capital, using terms such as "collective" cultural capital (Franklin, 2002; Span, 2002), "nondominant" cultural capital (Carter, 2003), "community cultural wealth" (Yosso, 2005), or "intercultural capital" (Núñez, 2009).

In the introduction to a special issue of *The Journal of African American History,* Franklin (2002) asserted that cultural capital can be defined more communally as "the sense of group consciousness and collective identity that serves as an economic resource for the financial and material support of business enterprises aimed at the advancement of an entire group" (p. 177). Franklin and his coauthors (see, for example, Span, 2002) used this definition and applied it to the way that African American people have given financial resources, time, or energy to educational institutions for the advancement of the entire group. For instance, Span (2002) analyzed the statements by George Washington Albright on Black education in Mississippi from 1861 to 1869, maintaining that African Americans' "enthusiasm for literacy and learning" provided the "cultural capital" necessary to establish the first Black schools in the state (p. 203).

In a theoretical and qualitative exploration into minority youth academic and ethnic identities in schooling, similar to Franklin and Span, Nasir and Saxe (2003) asserted a notion of "shifting cultural capital" that "evolves over social history through practices" (p. 17). This interpretation maintains that all communities have cultural capital and that this cultural capital advances over time as people in a community gain different opportunities and experiences.

Submitting an example of the way that cultural capital may develop, Carter (2003) propelled away from the high-status culture definition of cultural capital to argue that "dominant" and "nondominant" forms of cultural capital exist. Through in-depth interviews, she considered the "Black" cultural capital of African American youth and the ways in which their nondominant styles of interacting (language and clothing styles, for example) provided a form of currency in community settings, particularly among Black peers. Although this cultural capital was generally not valued in schools, this study featured the importance of Bourdieu's concept of field and suggested one of the ways that racially marginalized populations can navigate White spaces.

In a similar approach, Yosso (2005) tendered a theoretical progression of cultural capital, asserting a notion of "community cultural wealth" that teases out some of the distinctive forms of cultural capital that communities of color might possess. Although this type of cultural capital may often go unacknowledged or unrecognized in dominant cultures, Yosso's approach allows for a variety of kinds of cultural capital that students of color may bring into classrooms such as aspirational, navigational, social, linguistic, familial, and resistance capital. The implications of this interpretation maintain that schools and education can be developed to embrace these community cultural wealth forms of capital rather than continuing to reward the highbrow cultural capital that is often reinforced in educational settings.

Olneck's theoretical discussion (2000) connecting cultural capital with the tenets and practices of multicultural education, primarily at the K–12 level, posed a question as to whether multicultural education could transform cultural capital or at least the type of capital that is valued in educational institutions. Although the question remains, his work proffered a compelling shift away from a deficiency approach to cultural capital (that is, a student who does not possess the cultural capital valued in an institution is seen as somehow deficient).

At the postsecondary level, Núñez (2009) encouraged campuses to work toward what she calls "intercultural capital," where no one particular racial or ethnic group dominates campus norms. Intercultural capital is manifested as resources that promote or celebrate a diverse environment. Her structural equation modeling analysis of the longitudinal dataset, the Diverse Democracy Project, demonstrated that this intercultural capital positively related to students' academic self-confidence for second-year Latino students. Like in many other quantitative studies, parental education served as a proxy for cultural capital. Additionally, whether or not a parent took interest in the student's development was considered a marker of cultural capital. The major addition in this study was the "intercultural capital" variable, measured through a diversity curriculum factor that captured whether students took courses with content information on race, class, or gender.

In another statistical example, using the NELS dataset, Pearce and Lin (2005) explored differences in educational attainment of Chinese and White Americans, operationalizing cultural capital in a more nuanced way—as parental educational attainment, parental educational expectations, parental involvement in students' cultural activities and education, and parenting styles. The findings indicated that the cultural capital was related to academic achievement. But the cultural capital of Chinese Americans was evidenced to be rooted in their culture as a nondominant form of cultural capital while White American students appeared to possess cultural capital rewarded by schools, dominant forms of cultural capital (also see Pearce and Lin, 2007).

The scholarship, associated with the otherized forms of cultural capital, is more inclusive, maintaining that cultural capital is available to all and is perhaps even the possession of a group rather than an individual. The research in this area, save for a few studies (for example, Núñez, 2009; Pearce and Lin, 2005), is primarily qualitative, theoretical, or historical (see, for example, Carter, 2003; Franklin, 2002; Yosso, 2005). This tendency towards qualitative, theoretical, or historical work is no surprise, as methodologies in this vein are more interpretative and are often focused on nuances, meaning-making, and everyday lived experiences.

This line of work advances cultural capital, theorizing one step further than the contextually-valued cultural capital interpretation, particularly related to understanding the cultural capital of marginalized populations; it is a push away from the often used centrality of dominant cultural capital. Yet it may not be so big of a sea change as some may suspect with respect to Bourdieu's theoretical approach. Although Bourdieu primarily studied the dominant forms of cultural capital, exploring the way in which high-status groups continued to be privileged in social settings, his larger project was critical of the perpetuation of class inequality and stratification. Thus, the extension of cultural capital to explore nondominant forms of the concept may actually be a sharp insight into his larger project. That said, many of the otherized interpretations of cultural capital do not place cultural capital in the larger theory of social reproduction with which Bourdieu was involved.

Bourdieuian Framework Cultural Capital

Although the majority of studies using cultural capital as a theoretical or analytical tool employed this concept independent of Bourdieu's full theoretical apparatus, a growing number of scholars, particularly in higher education, have attempted to place cultural capital in Bourdieu's larger theory of social reproduction (Horvat, 1997; Lareau and Horvat, 1999; McDonough, 1997; Perna, 2000; Perna and Titus, 2005; Smrekar, 1996; Walpole, McDonough, Bauer, Gibson, Kanyi, and Toliver, 2005), using what some refer to as a "Bourdieuian framework" (Horvat, 2001). This line of research offers a different orientation toward cultural capital in which it is not so much knowledge and competence of *high-status* culture that encompasses the concept of cultural capital. Similar to the contextually-valued cultural capital interpretation, cultural capital in Bourdieu's full theory of social reproduction includes the way in which one can appropriate cultural resources (including knowledge, skills, competencies, and abilities) toward a particular end. The difference is that cultural capital is placed in the full theory of social reproduction, so it is often clearer how one form of cultural capital may be valued over another. Cultural capital, as part of a Bourdieuian framework, has been used in educational research to investigate such topics as family involvement in schooling or college enrollment (Lareau, 2000, 2003; Lareau and Horvat, 1999; Lee and Bowen, 2006; Perna and Titus, 2005); the way that marginalized students negotiate schooling (Monkman, Ronald, and Délimon Théramène, 2005); college access and college choice decision-making (Horvat, 1997; Martin and Spenner, 2009; McDonough, 1997; Walpole et al., 2005; Perna, 2000); educational outcomes such as social mobility (Zweigenhaft, 1993); and student activities in college (Salisbury, Umbach, Paulsen, and Pascarella, 2009). Scholars typically attempt to map cultural capital onto the full theory in two ways: along with social capital, and in conjunction with the concepts of field (the social setting or context, the "market" where cultural capital is given its value) and habitus (a series of dispositions or the range of options one sees as available).

Cultural capital and social capital. In a theoretical analysis of the uses of cultural and social capital in higher education research, Musoba and Baez (2009) argued that the "uncritical use" of Bourdieu's work may camouflage the importance of class structures and class struggles in the concepts. They asserted that Bourdieu's theoretical structure is first and foremost about understanding the perpetuation of inequality. This theoretical essay was largely a call for placing cultural capital in the larger theory of social reproduction and, more specifically, for using cultural capital in tandem with social capital.

In an attempt to discuss the differences in public or private preparatory school preparation for higher education, Zweigenhaft (1993) analyzed archival data to consider the cultural and social capital of Harvard and Radcliffe graduates who had previously attended elite preparatory schools or public schools. This study provided a compelling way to examine both the social origin and educational acquisition points of cultural and social capital. The findings indicated that although elite higher education experiences do bestow cultural and social capital, those who enter college with the forms of capital that are highly rewarded in that setting are privileged. Zweigenhaft essentially suggests that those with background cultural capital (primarily high status) more closely linked with prestigious educational institutions will be privileged over those who do not have this type of cultural capital. Although social and cultural capital were not entirely disentangled or differentiated in the theoretical discussion or the analysis, the study still demonstrated a graduated view into some of the ways that cultural and social capital may be initially acquired and then used to one's advantage throughout life.

Related to access to higher education, Perna's (2000) study using the NELS dataset found that for African American and Hispanic students, cultural capital was as important as ability when it came to their college enrollment decisions. The variables combined cultural capital with social capital, using such factors as high school quality; desegregation; high school region and location; educational expectations; and parental involvement, education, and encouragement. This operationalization of cultural capital included school-based and family-based notions of cultural capital, allowing for an understanding of social origin and educational acquisition of cultural knowledge, relationships, or competencies. Although cultural capital and social capital were well defined in their own right in the theoretical discussion, they were combined (as variables for social or cultural capital) in the statistical model for the study.

Later work by Perna and Titus (2005) used hierarchical linear modeling to examine parental involvement related to the likelihood of college enrollment and to analyze the NELS dataset; they found that parental involvement promotes college enrollment. The multilevel modeling in this project allowed for much more complexity in the operationalization of terms, and it permitted an examination of multiple fields at once (family, school, and so on). Here, variables for cultural capital were parental education, expectations for children's educational attainment, the primary language spoken at home, and involvement in children's cultural activities. Social capital variables represented different levels of parental involvement (parent-student, parent-parent, parent-school). This more dynamic exploration allowed cultural and social capital to stand together in that they do influence each other while maintaining their own qualities. Social capital (parental involvement) and cultural capital (parental education, expectations, and involvement in cultural activities) did relate to promoting students' college enrollment. This analysis allowed for another layer of complexity, maintaining that African American and Hispanic students may have fewer cultural and social resources at home and in the schools they often attend, highlighting between-school and background inequalities.

Also combining social and cultural capital, Martin and Spenner (2009) examined legacy admissions at Duke University and found that students whose parents attended the same elite institutions enter college with abundant social and cultural capital. Background social and cultural capital were combined through variables such as family income, parents' education level, and parents' occupational status. Additionally, the model included measurements of parents' and students' cultural activities and cultural resources (such as books and computers) in the home. It was not entirely clear, however, which variables were cultural capital variables and which variables were proxies for social capital.

Examining persistence from the first to the second year in community colleges, Wells's analysis of the NELS dataset (2008) indicated that students' ability to engage the valued cultural capital on a particular campus relates positively to their likelihood of persisting. Using Perna's (2000) operationalization of terms, Wells (2008) also defined cultural and social capital together to include such things as parents' education, parents' educational expectations, students' educational expectations, the importance of college attendance to the people around the student during high school, whether or not most or all of the student's high school friends planned to attend college, the quality of the high school attended (measured by the percentage of the student body that enrolled in postsecondary education), the extent to which the family had academic resources available at home, the extent to which test-preparation tools were used for the college transition, and a factor score that measured parents' involvement in the student's educational life.

Scholars like Salisbury, Umbach, Paulsen, and Pascarella (2009) have used cultural capital alongside social capital as a way to analyze students' in-college activities. In their analysis of the Wabash National Study on Liberal Arts Education, Salisbury and his colleagues (2009) investigated students' propensity for study abroad, finding that the cultural and social capital that students brought with them to college along with that gained in their first year related to their likelihood of studying abroad. In this model, variables of parental educational attainment blended with students' aspirations were used as measurements of background habitus. Like many other studies, the operationalization united social and cultural capital in the same variable. Then, proposing a nuanced depiction of acquired cultural capital in college, three different scales were included in the study, dealing with openness to diversity, high school involvement, and attitudes toward literacy.

A plurality of the studies using cultural and social capital together were quantitative, and many of them used the same dataset, the NELS. It is obviously one of the reasons why many of the ways the authors operationalized these concepts were similar: only particular variables were available in the dataset. One critique of work that discusses both cultural and social capital is that much of this work conflates the concepts, failing to differentiate them (McNeal, 1999). These studies often use social and cultural capital interchangeably as a marker for many of the less tangible forms of capital such as social relationships or the potential for them and cultural involvement, knowledge, or competence that is valued in a particular setting or the potential for it (see, for example, Perna, 2000; Saunders and Serna, 2004; Wells, 2008; Zweigenhaft, 1993). Often it is an issue with larger datasets, leading to the commonly used operationalization of parental education, income, and occupation as proxies for cultural *and* social capital, assuming that those students with parents who have a particular level of education (for example, a college degree) might have the potential for greater access to forms of cultural and social capital that are rewarded in educational settings (knowledge of how to apply for college, relationships with others who have degrees, for example). The problem is that social relationships are conceptually different from cultural knowledge, skills, or competencies. One could have cultural capital without necessarily possessing a great deal of social capital or vice versa. Hence, an important level of complexity is lost when these concepts are coalesced in this way. Multilevel statistical modeling might be one way to overcome some of these issues (see, for example, Perna and Titus, 2005).

Another challenge with many of the studies is that cultural and social capital are often removed from the Bourdieuian framework in which they should be situated. In other words, many of the studies that use social and cultural capital together as theoretical or analytical tools do not discuss the concepts of field or habitus. Yet without situating cultural and social capital in a particular context, it is difficult to fully understand the way that the "market" (the school, the family, the community) might reward particular manifestations of cultural and social knowledge, competencies, and skills.

Cultural capital, field, and habitus. Lareau (1987, 2003) and her colleagues have been instrumental in theoretically and empirically advancing cultural capital as connected to the larger theory of social reproduction (Lamont and Lareau, 1988; Lareau and Weininger, 2003; Weininger and Lareau, 2003). Lareau's ethnographic work (1987, 2003) provides a particularly useful study of cultural capital and the way it is manifested in primary and secondary education. Her earlier work explored family involvement in schools and the way that schools and teachers interpret this involvement, ultimately suggesting that particular cultural signals (active involvement on the part of parents, for example) are unequally rewarded by the schools, affecting children's educational experiences (Lareau, 1987). Lareau's more recent work (2003) used a cultural capital framework to investigate differences between class-based parenting styles (the way that parents did or did not structure their children's recreational time) and language styles (negotiating versus directing), examining the way that these familial habits perpetuate educational and social inequalities.

In a case study of parental involvement in the schooling of third graders, Lareau and Horvat (1999) discussed an example of a use of cultural capital that connects it to Bourdieu's larger theory of social reproduction. In their explanation of cultural capital, these scholars were careful to place cultural capital in a particular field (a third-grade classroom) and to note that cultural capital connects to habitus (a series of dispositions or skills related to culture). Students were demonstrated to experience educational rewards for the way in which their parents interacted with teachers and administrators.

In an examination of the social reproduction process in elite boarding schools, Cookson and Persell (1985) demonstrated the way that elite culture is perpetuated through college preparatory institutions, defining the field as the power structures in the United States more broadly. These schools, catering to the most socially elite, reward the cultural capital transmitted through families, and they perpetuate cultural capital, defined as codes of distinction that reinforce the dominant or subordinate hierarchy, associated with elite college and universities.

In an attempt to connect cultural capital to habitus, Dumais's (2002) research on gender differences in participation in cultural activities in schooling among eighth-grade boys and girls argued that female students and higher socioeconomic students may be more likely to be involved in cultural activities and that female students may be more encouraged to use their cultural capital for success in school. Although she used the NELS dataset much like other scholars, she operationalized cultural capital differently—as participation in the arts—using variables related to activities like borrowing books from a library, attending concerts of musical events, going to museums, or taking art-related classes outside school. Habitus was operationalized as occupational expectations. Dumais's analysis puts forward one of the more nuanced uses of the NELS dataset, attempting to operationalize terms in ways that are more consistent with Bourdieu's conceptual framework along with a cogent analysis of gender (also see Evans, 2009, for a gender analysis in the United Kingdom). This approach allowed for some confidence in the finding that cultural capital had a significant effect on the grades of female students. Dumais's later work (2006) examined teachers' evaluations (measured by a teacher questionnaire) of elementary students' abilities, using the Early Childhood Longitudinal Study to suggest that children's cultural activities did positively influence teachers' evaluations of language and mathematics abilities for low-income students. Parental expectations also had a positive effect on teachers' evaluations. Cultural capital was operationalized as students' cultural activities (dance lessons and music lessons, for example). Dumais argued through this evidence that the traditional definition of cultural capital may not be appropriate for young children, that there may not be many opportunities to demonstrate cultural capital at this level, and that other measures like sports or club participation should be included instead.

Bridging primary and secondary education with higher education, McDonough (1997) conducted qualitative research on the influences of high school counselors and families and the college choice process of students (also see McDonough, 1994; McDonough, Korn, and Yamasaki, 1997). In her book, McDonough considered what she deemed "organizational habitus" alongside the cultural capital of parents (as specified by parents' knowledge of the college admissions process), finding that the combination of organizational habitus (whether students are college bound or not) and background cultural capital (knowledge and understanding of college admissions) greatly influences students' college choice decision making. McDonough's work presents one of the applications of cultural capital on which many scholars, specifically in higher education, have built their understanding of cultural capital applications in research. But this work also initiated an important example of one way to study both sides of the acquisition process for cultural capital per Bourdieu's crafting of it, contrasting social origin (family) and education (schooling). In her later work, she examined the "field" of college admissions, exploring the increasing numbers of applications to elite colleges (McDonough, Ventresca, and Outcalt, 1999). This analysis demonstrates the conflict of middle-class families' attempting to secure their status and power through placing their children in these elite colleges, creating a habitus associated with the vital importance of attending an elite college.

Horvat has been at the forefront of creating a bridge between Bourdieu's framework and racial inequality in education (Horvat, 2001, 2003). She extended her work to the study of inequality in higher education (Horvat, 1997, 2001, 2003; Lareau and Horvat, 1999), maintaining that another important aspect of the college decision-making process is the social and psychological experiences that a student has before entering college. In her longitudinal qualitative study, Horvat (1997) explored the way that these precollege experiences shaped Black female high school students' college choice process, suggesting that the cultural capital and habitus of students related to their sense of support and their feelings of fit with a particular college. In this case, students tended to choose institutions that had a visible group of other Black students. Horvat's (2001) Bourdieuian analysis of longitudinal case studies of high school seniors' college choice processes demonstrated the way that students' cultural capital and habitus greatly influence their college enrollment decisions. Her observations both inside and outside schools allowed for the inclusion of both social origin and educational acquisitions of cultural capital and for the placement of cultural capital in the idea of field.

Building on Horvat's (1997) work, Nora (2004) developed and analyzed the Survey of Attitudes and Behaviors Influencing College Choice, in part to explore the way cultural capital and habitus that students brought with them to college continued to influence their satisfaction during college. The results suggested that cultural capital and habitus were related to students' perceptions of acceptance, fit, and comfort on campus. Nora's four-stage quantitative analysis identified factors associated with habitus and cultural capital that could be used in other studies. For instance, items were included in the survey that reflect students' attitudes and behaviors related to such issues as their background, goals, perceived institutional support, and extracurricular experiences.

Also aimed at understanding college access, Walpole and her colleagues (2005) interviewed African American and Latino students, framing knowledge of college admissions exams as a marker for cultural capital and habitus; the findings indicated that many students lacked knowledge of these exams and there was often little support in their school systems to help them get this information. Although this approach dealt more with culturally relevant knowledge than skills or abilities, it provides a compelling example of how a Bourdieuian framework can be applied to persistent questions of educational inequality.

Considering the implications of cultural capital for college student retention from a theoretical approach, Tierney (1999) argued that cultural capital, particularly the three types (institutionalized, objectified, and embodied), along with habitus could be instructive, suggesting that minority students could *learn* the cultural capital that majority students may have already inherited to be successful in college. Ultimately, Tierney's (1999) point was to shift the burden of responsibility for the success of students of color from individual students to institutions, suggesting that institutions should be more adaptive to students' cultural norms. This angle on cultural capital connects well with the otherized interpretations, shifting some of the focus away from understanding only those forms of cultural capital or habitus dominant in a particular field.

Conclusion

Over the past thirty years, cultural capital has permeated the research in both primary/secondary and postsecondary education. Scholars, many of whom were primarily concerned with issues of educational inequality, have interpreted and used Bourdieu's cultural capital as well as his other relevant theoretical concepts in four different ways. Bourdieu's concepts have been employed as everything from theoretical frameworks to analytical tools in the extant research studies. And it does not seem that this trend of contemplating cultural capital acquisition, appropriation, and educational rewards will slow anytime soon. With this factor in mind, I turn my attention toward synthesizing this body of scholarship, contemplating the strengths and limitations, the promises and pitfalls, of applications and interpretations of cultural capital.

"Strikes and Gutters": Examining Applications and Interpretations of Cultural Capital

ULTURAL CAPITAL AT ITS BEST can provide a "complex and far-reaching conceptual framework to deal with the phenomenon of cultural and social selection" (Lamont and Lareau, 1988, p. 154). Contrarily, has the "promise" of cultural capital largely gone "unfilled," as Kingston (2001) asserted in his analysis of extant research using the concept? This chapter explores both the merits and limitations of the interpretations and applications of cultural capital in educational research.

The Merits of Cultural Capital in Educational Research

In education, cultural capital has the hope of providing an explanation of the way that cultural and social privilege, at least based on class, is perpetuated and manifested in schools and higher education institutions. Additionally, Bourdieu's framework sheds light on one of the ways that stratification and inequality are maintained. The notion of cultural capital appears to have some noteworthy aspects, given the increased use of it as either an analytical or theoretical framework in educational research. This section explores the merits and research implications of Bourdieu's cultural capital, given the use of it in scholarship in education.

Beyond Human Capital Theories: The Less Tangible Aspects of Socioeconomic Inequality

Using an economic metaphor, Bourdieu considerably expanded the notion of "capital" and the way that capital can be acquired and exchanged in educational institutions. Cultural capital goes beyond physical, tangible financial and economic capital. But he also significantly reached beyond the notion of human capital, primarily associated with skills and knowledge. Human capital theory stemmed in large part from econometric research in the 1960s (Becker, 1993; Schultz, 1961). The premise of human capital theories is that one is able to weigh the costs and benefits of earning a college degree, for example, and willing to forgo short-term economic gains for more lucrative long-term gains. Action, in human capital theory, is intentional and goal oriented. Human capital theory assumes a rational choice model where one's action is instrumental, action is geared toward a particular end, ideally one has full information available, and one has the ability to weigh options to make the best decision. Upward mobility and human agency are the center of attention in human capital theory (Musoba and Baez, 2009).

Cultural capital extends those theories that use an economic capital metaphor, pushing away from rational choice models (those models that assume intentional, individual action and full information and for which one can calculate costs and benefits of one's actions). Rather, through the examination of a less tangible form of capital, associated with cultural mores and norms, Bourdieu considered the way that the social structure influences individual action in tacit ways. Although one may still have some intention or goal with one's action, this action may be directed in implicit, seemingly unconscious ways by habitual sets of norms and practices (tastes, preferences) that are socially embedded. Thus, Bourdieu could unmask the subtle way that privilege, power, and domination are perpetuated and transferred. Cultural capital allows for the exposure of cumulative advantage that one acquires through *both* social origin and education.

Indeed, cultural capital and the larger framework in which it is rooted (including the concepts of field, habitus, and social capital), permit an investigation between the individual and the group as well as between the group and the social structure. Although financial capital and human capital theories are primarily directed at understanding individual action, the gaze of cultural capital is at least partially oriented toward larger social structural issues. Human capital is placed primarily in the labor market. Cultural capital, on the other hand, imparts a consideration of both family background and social institutions (Lamont and Lareau, 1988). Musoba and Baez (2009) captured this distinction in their analysis of cultural and social capital use in higher education: "Unlike the selfishly motivated, upwardly mobile individual premised by human-capital theories, Bourdieu sees cultural capital as becoming more and more a new basis of social domination, particularly as education becomes more and more important for economic and professional success. Just as economic capital cannot function as capital until it is linked to an economic apparatus, so cultural capital cannot be constituted as capital until it is inserted into the fields . . . such as the school and the family" (p. 156). It is through this attention to social domination that one can begin to uncover the system of power and privilege that Bourdieu attempted to uncover through his theoretical and empirical work.

Interactions Between the Individual and Structure: Power, Domination, and Inequality

The sociology of education contains a commonly used differentiation between functional and conflict theories (see, for example, Collins, 1971). Functional theories, chiefly rooted in Davis and Moore's (1945) occupational stratification research, maintain that occupational positions are functionally necessary for the social order, that occupations require particular skills, and that these positions must be filled by people who naturally have these skills or by those who have been trained in them.

The problem with functional theories, among other things, is that they normalize inequality as necessary to sustain the social order. Applied to education, a functionalist approach essentially means that inequalities in educational access or outcomes are not necessarily problematic but emblematic of the necessarily preordained set of status positions: only so many high-status positions exist, and education must therefore not credential more people than the positions available for them to fill. Education, then, serves the purpose of reproducing the functional social order, channeling people into the appropriate level of educational attainment (that is, many should be channeled out to maintain order) and placing people into their "rightful" status.

Conflict theories, on the other hand, elucidate the *process* of stratification. Namely, conflict theories point to the group conflict that occurs amid unequal social conditions (Collins, 1971). The concentration on process allows for a deeper consideration of the way that some groups are continually privileged over others. Education, in the case of conflict theories, becomes a place where status cultures are learned or acquired, conflict between status groups can be demonstrated, the process of the perpetuation of privilege and power can be studied, and education has the potential in ideal circumstances for altering the perpetuation of status, power, and privilege. It is within this tradition of conflict theory that Bourdieu's cultural capital emerged.

The gaze of cultural capital tends to be toward structural forces, emphasizing the way that privilege can be perpetuated among individuals and through institutions. This emphasis on social-structural inequalities and the way that these inequalities are reproduced is important in exposing the larger system of power and domination in a particular field. Applying Bourdieu's theoretical construction to higher education, Horvat (2001) maintained that cultural capital is "especially useful in revealing the power dynamics that support current status arrangements in higher education" (pp. 196–197). The same could be said for primary and secondary education.

The way that Bourdieu captured these power dynamics is through stressing the importance of interactions and relationships between "institutions and individuals, culture, and social biography" (Horvat, 2001, p. 234). For instance, McDonough's (1997) case studies of students' college choice processes provided evidence of many moments when students interacted with their high school counselors in such a way as to mirror the larger system of power and domination. That is, high school counselors afforded students only the options that they saw as appropriate for a student from a particular location in the existing social structure. These interactions, between counselors and students in various secondary schools, divulge an educational system that privileges students from higher socioeconomic backgrounds.

Bourdieu's cultural capital challenges the notion of meritocracy in education and does so in a compelling and useful way. Bourdieu (1979a/1984) ultimately maintained that educational institutions are most often created by and for the elite, the dominant class in a particular field. Those who are not in this dominant class must contend with the norms, values, attitudes, and behaviors that the dominant class maintains are appropriate in that setting.

Thus, "social distinctions [are transformed] into educational distinctions, which are then socially constructed as distinctions of merit" (McDonough, Ventresca, and Outcalt, 1999, p. 5). Bourdieu brought to light the way in which this process of apparent meritocracy, through interactions, occurs.

Rather than earlier, more functionalist notions of social reproduction (see, for example, Bowles and Gintis, 1976) that implied an almost mechanistic acceptance of inequality on the part of individuals,[4] Bourdieu's theoretical view leaves room for the individual to interact with the social structure. The interaction-centered characteristics of Bourdieu's theoretical development is in part what helps to bridge what Horvat (2001) deemed the "agency/structure gap" that often permeates thought about social reproduction (also see, Lamont and Lareau, 1988). Technically, one could become conscious and reflective of one's cultural capital and then respond by trying to acquire more of the kind of cultural capital that is valued in a particular setting. Although it might be quite difficult to achieve, the *potential* for it does open the door to agency that might be closed in functionalist social reproduction theories. In effect, Bourdieu tasks those who use his work with uncovering the often concealed "systematic mechanisms that perpetuate patterns of domination and subordination" (Horvat, 2001, p. 201). The effort of discovering tacit domination and subordination is in itself an act of agency.

Bourdieu's Sociology: Linking Theory and Data and the Macro- and Microlevels

A few implications for research, across methodological approaches, can be garnered from Bourdieu's work. Bourdieu's scholarship represents a convincing example of an iterative, interactive process between theory development and empirical evidence. His work was neither the type of thought that was removed from practice and everyday experience or so evidence based that it was atheoretical and separated from larger social issues. Rather, Bourdieu, through his theoretical development and the empirical evidence he collected to support and evolve this framework, established an example of an innovative way that theory can be used in research. The scientific method, increasingly encouraged in the study of education (as in experimental designs and many quantitative analyses), would generally maintain that a researcher must begin with a theoretical idea, a hypothesis, and then test it to show evidence to support or negate the theory. In qualitative or interpretive research, grounded theory (see Charmaz, 2005; Glaser and Strauss, 1967), for example, works in the opposite direction, often for the purpose of studying topics for which there are few theories. In grounded theory research, one would start by collecting data and then, through careful and systematic data analysis, craft a theory connected with this data. Bourdieu found a way to elegantly avoid the limitations of the use of theory in both of these brands of research methodology. He began with a "grand theory," using existing philosophical work and his criticisms of it to guide his methodology. Then through data collection, he continued to evolve his theoretical understanding, rooting it in empirical evidence. But he also continued to connect his theoretical reasoning with larger social theories beyond the data in his empirical studies, which may call for scholars who adapt Bourdieu's theoretical structure to do the same.

Lareau's (2003) ethnographic work examining the interactions among families, schools, and children relative to the way that they structure recreational time represents an exemplar of the way that Bourdieu related theory and data in his work. Lareau began with Bourdieu's theoretical apparatus in mind, particularly concentrating on cultural capital and the fields of families and schools. Then as she analyzed her data, Bourdieu's cultural capital evolved into two parenting styles: concerted cultivation (associated with very structured free time for children aimed at "cultivating" the student toward continued social mobility) and the accomplishment of natural growth (connected to unstructured playtime for children aimed at nurturing their creativity and independence). Each style exemplified a particular set of cultural capital resources and the ability of a family to appropriate that capital in schooling. Ultimately, this work employed Bourdieu's theoretical framework and extended it.

Perhaps before his time, Bourdieu was a consummate mixed methodologist. One of his largest works, *Distinction: A Social Critique of the Judgment of Taste* (1979a/1984), prefaced his survey creation with hundreds of interviews (692 total). He continued to evolve his survey instrument through these interviews, collecting survey responses from 1,217 French people in 1963. Likewise, Bourdieu's argument offers insight into both micro- and macrolevel issues, shifting "our focus away from looking exclusively at how individuals navigate the system of . . . education, and [directing] our attention to exploring how the system itself reflexively structures individuals' pathways" (Horvat, 2001, p. 201). Bourdieu's theoretical and empirical work constantly seesaws between the individual and the social structure. Yet despite the fact that many scholars have employed Bourdieu's theoretical model, few have followed the mixed methods approach that he took with his work. In the pool of 105 studies reviewed for this monograph, only three identified the research as using a mixed methodology. Even among those who did label the research this way, one aspect of the methodology was often unclear. For instance, the study might mention that interviews were conducted, but the methodology for this part of the research was not described and it was not clear how the qualitative and quantitative aspects of the work interacted.

Lessons from Cultural Capital in the Extant Educational Research

The use of Bourdieu's framework and cultural capital in particular in educational research has highlighted many issues of educational inequality that may not have otherwise been identified. Socioeconomic background (income level) does not explain the way that class-based inequality is perpetuated. As Lareau (2003) noted in *Unequal Childhoods: Class, Race, and Family Life*, some students are "born on third base but believe they hit a triple" (p. 12). Cultural capital helps to explain why some kids are seemingly destined to hit a triple while others cannot seem to get to first base, despite their efforts to swing the bat.

It has become no secret that the simple examination of income levels does not adequately explain class-based disparities in the larger social context (Conley, 1999/2010; Shapiro, 2004). Some people, beyond the simple numeric inequalities, are continually put in positions of dominance and power. Although this disparity in power and privilege relates to monetary inequalities, more is certainly involved in capturing the full picture. For example, what about the hidden "rules" of engagement in an educational institution that some students seem to know and with which others seem unfamiliar? What about the tacit way that the clothes one wears, the music one listens to, and the food one brings for lunch privilege that person over others? What about the way that some students' after-school or extracurricular activities seem to be more important in terms of their academic success than their ability to recall class materials? How might teachers' judgments and expectations of their students, often based on nonacademic characteristics, affect students' ability to succeed in that educational setting? Cultural capital has helped to put forward answers to these questions and more.

Attempting to summarize succinctly the remarkable findings of 105 studies is no easy task. Notwithstanding this challenge and the limitations that I outline below, I recall some of the significant conclusions of these studies. It is important to do so because the use of cultural capital in educational research has helped to highlight the way that students' backgrounds, not just in socioeconomic terms but relative to their families' tastes, preferences, norms, and way of spending recreational time, affect their educational chances. Additionally, this work has accented the often implicit judgments that teachers, faculty, or administrators may use to measure students' "ability," even if these judgments are not based on actual ability. Finally, this work has stressed the way in which learned tastes, preferences, or norms may influence educational decisions in ways that often go unnoticed. This work helps to explain the way that some students seem entitled to educational privilege while others appear to be perpetually disadvantaged throughout their educational careers.

Research in the highbrow cultural capital definitional groups presents compelling evidence of the rewards afforded to those who demonstrate knowledge and competence associated with high-status or elite cultural activities. The possession of high-status cultural knowledge or competence has been correlated with academic achievement, grades, and general academic success in primary and secondary schooling (Aschaffenburg and Maas, 1997; DiMaggio, 1982; English, 2002; Katsillis and Rubinson, 1990; Roscigno and Ainsworth-Darnell, 1999). For higher education, participation in highbrow cultural activities or knowledge of and competence in these activities have been evidenced to affect college access (Karen, 1991; Tierney, 2002), students' choice of college institution (Goyette and Mullen, 2006), students' experiences after enrollment in college (Pascarella et al., 2004), and the likelihood of students' attending graduate school (DiMaggio and Mohr, 1985).

The scholarship that identifies cultural capital as cultural knowledge, competence, skills, or abilities that are valued in a particular educational context (contextually-valued cultural capital) suggests that subtle symbols of one's social location matter relative to educational success. For example, teachers often reward students' noncognitive abilities (background characteristics, work habits, appearance, and so on), which affects students' achievement in school (Farkas et al., 1990). The type of parental and family involvement teachers and administrators recognize affects students' achievement (Cheadle, 2008). Related to higher education, evidence suggests that students' knowledge of the educational system writ large influences their decisions about college attendance (Freeman, 1997; Valadez, 1993). Yet, once students enroll in college, not having the culturally relevant knowledge or competence may negatively influence their sense of self (Aries and Seider, 2005).

Using the Bourdieuian framework or at least aspects of it (including field, habitus, and social capital), scholars identified some of the ways that social background influences educational success. Privileged social origins can bestow a cumulative advantage to students over their educational career (Martin and Spenner, 2009; Salisbury et al., 2009; Zweigenhaft, 1993). For instance, everything from parenting styles (Lareau, 2003) to the way that teachers interpret family involvement in schools (Lareau, 1987, 2000; Lareau and Horvat, 1999) may influence students' educational outcomes. Parental involvement in education, at least that involvement recognized by teachers and administrators, may promote college enrollment (Perna and Titus, 2005). Some social origins may lead students to be enrolled in secondary schools that encourage students to attend college, while other high schools do not (McDonough, 1997). Additionally, one's cultural knowledge and competence can influence college decision-making processes (Perna, 2000). It is possible that some students have more knowledge of college admissions exams, for example, which affords them privileges in the college admissions process (Walpole et al., 2005). After a student enrolls in college, his or her ability to engage the cultural knowledge or competence valued on campus positively relates to his or her likelihood of persisting (Wells, 2008). Yet many students, particularly students of color, do not have this knowledge, which influences their sense of fit or comfort on campus (Nora, 2004). With this factor in mind, perhaps underrepresented or marginalized students could learn or be taught the cultural capital valued in higher education institutions, as some scholars have recommended (Collier and Morgan, 2008; Pascarella et al., 2004; Tierney, 1999).

Those studies that I have grouped as employing a nondominant (otherized) interpretation of cultural capital indicate that the notion of cultural capital could be used to advance the background-, familial-, or community-oriented cultural knowledge, competences, skills, and abilities of often marginalized groups (Carter, 2003; Nasir and Saxe, 2003; Núñez, 2009; Olneck, 2000; Yosso, 2005). Extending the applications of cultural capital to racial inequality suggests high-status cultural knowledge and competence can be a vehicle to mitigate racial inequality (Kalmijn and Kraaykamp, 1996). The argument goes that if students of color could acquire knowledge of the cultural capital valued in educational institutions, they might be able to more successfully navigate these institutions (Collier and Morgan, 2008; Pascarella et al., 2004; Tierney, 1999). But evidence suggests that African American and Hispanic students may have fewer cultural and social resources at home and in the schools they often attend, suggesting that some students will enter college at a disadvantage relative to cultural capital acquisition (Perna and Titus, 2005). These findings should be viewed with some caution, however, as some contradictory results have been found; Roscigno and Ainsworth-Darnell (1999), for example, found that Black and lower-income students received fewer educational rewards (higher test scores) from their involvement in high-status cultural activities than did their White and high-income peers. Thus, not only are some students coming into educational institutions without the cultural capital advantaged in these settings but, even if they do acquire this cultural capital, they may receive fewer rewards for it than do their White peers. Other evidence indicates that cultural capital might be as important as academic ability when it comes to college enrollment (Perna, 2000). All told, it seems that the jury is still out when it comes to the application of cultural capital to racial inequality in education.

Although noteworthy achievements exist relative to the application and interpretation of cultural capital in educational research, important limitations also need further exploration. The point of highlighting potential challenges to the concept and interpretation of cultural capital in educational research is not meant to imply that cultural capital should not be used or explored in empirical research. Rather, these limitations should be considered and addressed in future work to make the study of cultural capital, or the use of it as an analytical tool, more robust.

Substantive Limitations of Cultural Capital

Cultural capital is limited substantively for several reasons: (1) the economic metaphor is restrictive; (2) the creation and maintenance of moral boundaries are too often not considered; (3) emphasis is limited on homogeneous class-based privileges in a pluralistic society like the United States; (4) race and gender are not well studied using a cultural capital framework as it is currently theorized; and (5) cultural capital, if misused, can become a deficiency model, blaming "deficient" students for what is the fault of the stratified social structure.

The Economic Metaphor of Cultural Capital

The economic metaphor implicit in the notion of cultural capital could limit the topics that could be studied using this theoretical idea. The economic metaphor highlights the potential market value of cultural signals. It maintains that one could exchange these cultural signals in a particular marketplace (field, in Bourdieu's language) for privileges or particular rewards. If educational institutions are the field, one could exchange cultural capital, manifested as linguistic capabilities, particular ways of dressing or acting, tastes in music and food, and so on for rewards such as increased teacher expectations, higher academic achievement, a longer list of college options relative to choices about college, or acceptance in a particular educational setting. An economic metaphor assumes that one's primary motivation is the exchange of goods, services, or money or, in the case of cultural capital, the exchange of cultural knowledge, competences, skills, or abilities for educational outcomes. Individualism and utilitarianism are embedded in the economic metaphor.

This economic metaphor involves a means-ends assumption that could be quite individualistic, assuming that one's primary goal is to maximize one's options. Although Bourdieu's theoretical ideas are not limited to include only the "utilitarian pursuit of gaining an advantage," the economic metaphor suggests that the exchange and profit seeking are at least "interested" in earning material or symbolic "profits" (Olneck, 2000, p. 319; Bourdieu and Wacquant, 1992; Swartz, 1997). Despite the tacit assumption of rational, utilitarian decision making in the economic metaphor, Bourdieu's genesis of cultural capital maintains that "it is important that most action appears to be disinterested, in that it is not consciously intended to, nor does it appear to, result in advantage to the actor" (Olneck, 2000, p. 319). This underground enactment of cultural capital may have been intentional on Bourdieu's part, a way to tender insight into the complexities of privilege, status, and power. But the interpretations of Bourdieu's theoretical notions in educational research have not reflected this complexity. Those scholars who have recommended that college students be coached in acquiring and appropriating cultural capital (see Collier and Morgan, 2008; Pascarella et al., 2004; Tierney, 1999), for example, have generally not made clear that key components of "exchanging" cultural capital in education are the knowledge and skills to be able to make this exchange appear natural, unplanned, disinterested, and not like an exchange at all. It is not enough to simply *acquire* the skills, knowledge, or competence; one must also have the knowledge of how to make it seem natural, unplanned, and disinterested (that is, have the ability to appropriate it). For instance, Collier and Morgan's (2008) discussion of the importance of helping students master the role of "college student" as a way to teach students college-relevant cultural capital (defined as highbrow culture) does not describe the way that this role must be enacted so as to make indistinct the utilitarian exchange of cultural knowledge and skills for educational rewards. It simply may not be enough to act like a "college student"; one adept at appropriating the cultural capital associated with this role must also be proficient at masking the way in which the signals associated with this role (linguistic competence, knowledge of particular cultural artifacts, ways of dressing, and so on) are being exchanged.

Bourdieu's intent with cultural capital, and his work more generally, was to expose the way in which social stratification, particularly class-based inequality, was acquired, perpetuated, and reinforced. Do certain aspects of social reproduction remain unequivocal to a means-end, utilitarian, market-based metaphor? Some slippage is apparent, for example, in the application of a more communal idea like culture to the individualism and utilitarianism implicit in the economic metaphor of cultural capital. Culture and the resulting cultural capital construct are more communal—something linked to social norms, values, tastes, and preferences that are rooted in a larger social structure. Bourdieu's project might be to highlight this social structure and the more communal forms of capital. Yet the economic metaphor itself is difficult to untangle from its individualistic, means-end, instrumental assumptions.

The individualistic assumptions inherent in the economic metaphor may be at the heart of some scholars' concerns that cultural capital has not been well adapted to the study of "minoritized" populations (Gilbourn, 2005). Although some have attempted to explore more communal versions of cultural capital that are applicable to people of color in the United States, for example (see Franklin, 2002; Span, 2002), more frequently those attempting to consider communal cultural capital must ultimately unleash the concept, at least in part, from the individualism assumed by the economic metaphor. Yosso's (2005) discussion of community cultural wealth, for instance, still uses "capital" as a metaphor, but she extends cultural capital to include more communal ideas such as family capital or resistance capital (associated with group resistance).

Group membership or group identification may not link well with an economic metaphor, given the individualism assumed by the economic link. Some social groups may exist with which one can exchange goods, services, financial capital, or some other reward to be involved (for example, golf country clubs and some high-status community groups). But some groupings are structured around less economic terms. For example, racial groups cannot necessarily be categorized in terms of "capital," where one could exchange something for membership. Rather, some groups, like racial groups in many cases, are rooted in ascriptive categories or behavioral norms. Behavior may not always connect well with an exchange-oriented metaphor. As racist society works, one who appears Black may act "White," attempting to be incorporated into the dominant society. Yet, gaining full membership in the "White" racial group is limited, based as it is on physical appearance. So although behavior *could* in some cases act as a form of capital (something that could be exchanged), the limits imposed on full group membership are *outside* an economic construction, which in part has to do with moral boundaries (see next page and also Lamont, 1992).

Additionally, the economic metaphor sets up at least some material dependency in the study of cultural capital. The notion of markets, exchanges, products, and instrumental goal orientation connects well with those aspects of social life that can be objectified. Bourdieu does, in my estimation, provide a compelling and persuasive study of the way that seemingly intangible aspects of one's lifestyle or tastes are objectified and treated similarly to material objects. Yet some topics (identity, for example) are not well represented as a "possession of capital." Identity is so close to home, in a manner of speaking, that it is *more* than a possession (see, for example, Torres, Howard-Hamilton, and Cooper, 2003; Winkle-Wagner, 2009b). Further, the principle of social integration involved in identity development is not a market- or interests-based principle. Identity initiates in the locale of norms, culture, values, and attitudes—perhaps in the realm of moral boundaries—not necessarily in the market primarily concerned with the transference and possession of capital.

Moral Boundaries and Cultural Capital

As Lamont (1992) summarized in her noteworthy qualitative comparative study of French and American upper-middle-class males, Bourdieu "greatly underestimated the importance of moral boundaries" (p. 5). Although not included in the sample of studies in the previous chapter because it did not include a treatment of education, Lamont's study expounded an important extension and critique of Bourdieu's theory of cultural capital. Lamont's primary critique was that Bourdieu focused more on high-status cultural signals than the creation of symbolic boundaries (that is, cultural boundaries). Bourdieu emphasized class and cultural differences based on commonly understood class categories, according to Lamont, while almost wholly ignoring preferences that one considers to be moral—why someone feels that someone is "one of us" or "not one of us." Group membership or in-group and out-group configurations may or may not link well with an economic metaphor, because inclusion and exclusion are often based on morality. Social groups may exist with which one can exchange goods, services, financial capital, or some other reward to be involved (golf country clubs or some high-status community group, for example). But, some groups are simply not structured around economic terms. Lamont (1992) found that American men in particular created moral boundaries more than they referenced a commonly understood cultural category of class. The moral boundaries may at times correspond with class boundaries, but in the U.S. context, moral boundaries are often also apparent in categories such as race and gender.

Morality and moral boundary making have long been ways to segregate and stratify people based on race (see, for example, Banton, 1998). Racial groups cannot necessarily be categorized in terms of "capital," as I alluded to above, where one could exchange something for membership. Rather, some groups, like racial groups in many cases, maintain the boundaries of their membership through notions of morality. That is, racial groups are often centered on the idea that those in a particular group have some implicit *moral* or normative connection. This idea has been one of the foundations of racism, the idea that those who appear different from the dominant group (White in the American context) are somehow considered inferior or morally deviant (Banton, 1998).

Arguably, cultural capital could be revised to include categories such as race or gender in a way that better answers to moral boundaries. But the theory has not been extensively redeveloped in this way beyond Lamont's study (1992), and that study did not stress racialized or gendered analysis. Bourdieu's notion of cultural capital is predominantly applied to categories like race or gender, often without consideration for the limitations of this application or without making salient that cultural capital is most readily linked to class stratification and class culture.

If one is looking to use an expanded notion of cultural capital that may allow for moral boundaries relative to race, gender, or class, Lamont and Lareau's (1988) definition of cultural capital may best include moral in- and out-grouping: "cultural capital is institutionalized, i.e., widely shared, high-status cultural signals (attitudes, preferences, formal knowledge, behaviors, goals, and credentials) used for social and cultural exclusion" (p. 156). The consideration of inclusion and exclusion links to moral boundaries in a way that many interpretations of Bourdieu's definition do not. Yet there certainly is room for continued theoretical development of cultural capital connected with creation and maintenance of moral boundaries.

Homogeneous Class-Based Privilege and a Pluralistic Society

The class-based framework in which cultural capital was crafted is somewhat limited, in part because of the initiation of Bourdieu's theoretical analysis in the context of France and in part because of the limitations to class analysis more generally. Bourdieu's (1979a/1984) cultural capital originated in part in his study of comparisons among French middle, working, and upper classes. "Class" in this case was largely defined as socioeconomic status. Although Bourdieu in many ways advocated a Weberian notion of "class" as a type of status group that could encompass categories like race, gender, religion, or other markers of group membership, his operationalization and theorizing of class was more closely linked to socioeconomic status than they were to other categories. In France and many European nations, clearly defined class cultures were (and perhaps are) often associated with high-status cultural signals (see, for example, Lamont, 1992). I question whether the assumption of clearly defined boundaries around classes exists in the same way in pluralistic contexts like the United States (also see Lamont, 1992; Lamont and Lareau, 1988; Kingston, 2000, 2001).

The way that Bourdieu (1979a/1984) studied class boundaries in his landmark *Distinction: A Social Critique of the Judgment of Taste,* for example, may not be relevant to the United States. As a conflict theorist, Bourdieu studied class in a way that can be linked to a Marxist class dichotomy (dominant-subordinate), where class is "a formation, on to which, in addition to culture can be attributed a class consciousness and struggle" (Musoba and Baez, 2009, p. 177). In his survey, Bourdieu asked questions that assumed that particular music or other art forms (classical music, opera, ballet, for example) were associated with high-status culture. The problem in transferring this assumption to a country context like the United States, for example, is that people who would be classified as belonging to the high-status classes have a diverse variety of tastes that often overlap with those in lower socioeconomic (and status) positions (Kingston, 2001). For instance, a high-status person might prefer to listen to opera but also enjoy country music. Tastes are not as one dimensional in a pluralistic context.

Regarding the high-status category as an example of the difficulty in cross-country application of Bourdieu's work, potentially different high-status class cultural representations also exist in the different geographic regions in the United States. In other words, the lifestyle of those in the higher socioeconomic social strata in various regions may incorporate different activities, styles of dress, styles of music, or preferences in food. On the East Coast, perchance, high socioeconomic status is partially signified by attending elite boarding schools or preparatory academies followed by Ivy League or elite liberal arts colleges. In the Midwest, "elite" postsecondary institutions for many students may be state universities because Ivy League institutions simply are not that geographically accessible. Bourdieu would say it is because the East Coast has a more dominant position in creating the valued cultural capital. Although it may be true in this example, I continue to wonder whether different patterns of high-status lifestyle really are geographically linked. Similar patterns may emerge, but they may have slight (or in some cases large) variations based on region. And some accounting is necessary for the geographic mobility of people moving from one part of the country to another. Thus, the use of cultural capital without first reframing the theoretical scaffolding to make it relevant to the nuances and variation of a pluralistic society like the United States may be inappropriate.

Besides the variation in tastes and lifestyles in a pluralistic context like the United States, the attention to class, particularly those interpretations that maintain cultural capital as connected to highbrow cultural signals (see, for example, DiMaggio, 1982; DiMaggio and Mohr, 1985), may be problematic in advanced industrial countries. Cultural hierarchies have "dramatically blurred in advanced capitalist societies" (Holt, 1998, p. 5), and one reason is "seriality and mass reproduction," meaning that culturally related products (objectified cultural capital) have become more accessible (p. 5). For example, reproductions of what would once be considered "highbrow artwork" are now accessible to the masses. Although one could conceivably still distinguish between those objects that were originals and those that were reproductions, the accessibility of these objects makes class distinctions harder to immediately distinguish.

Additionally, the norms associated with what is culturally "in" and "out" in the objectified sense of cultural capital are continually in flux in advanced industrial nations like the United States. But "objectified cultural capital can operate effectively only within a stable cultural hierarchy" (Holt, 1998, p. 5). Thus, as the cultural hierarchy becomes less stable, or less outwardly identifiable, the study of objectified cultural capital becomes muddier and less convincing. Nonetheless, many studies still examine objectified cultural capital through measurement of the number of books in one's home or ownership of particular artwork or similar artifacts as if there were clearly defined high-status and low-status goods—all of which is not to imply that the objectified cultural capital exchange may not occur in American society. It has possibly gone "underground," where the rules and regulations of what is culturally relevant in a particular context are less and less clear (that is, those cultural artifacts identified as "high status" are constantly changing to keep them less accessible). It is also very likely that embodied cultural capital is more prominent.

Embodied cultural capital would imply an investigation of "consumption practices themselves" (Holt, 1998, p. 6). One such cultural practice can be exemplified in the study of education. For instance, studies that include culturally relevant lessons or involvement in cultural classes (such as music lessons or art classes) attempt to capture this practice (see, for example, Cheadle, 2008), but clear class distinctions are also murkier for embodied cultural capital in the form of education. As primary and secondary education has become compulsory and higher education has become more accessible, it is more difficult to measure "high" and "low" class culture through educational credentials. Yet it is precisely how the majority of empirical studies have at least in part operationalized background cultural capital as the educational attainment (credentials) of a student's parents. Scholarship that examines gradations in status associated with particular schools (for example, private education versus public education) may be more relevant in explaining embodied cultural capital (see Cookson and Persell, 1985; Zweigenhaft, 1993).

Related to education, the absence of a clearly defined, homogenous, high-status class-based culture in the United States is problematic for cultural capital use. In their analysis of educational research studies that employ cultural capital, Lareau and Weininger (2003) posed a similar argument, suggesting that "the association of cultural capital . . . with 'highbrow' cultural activities . . . may well have been intended to apply only to the French context" (p. 579). Bourdieu's theory assumes that those with power in education (teachers, administrators, professors, for example) recognize value and perpetuate high-status culture. This statement is a key component of the theory because those with power are the ones who would reward or sanction students for possessing or lacking cultural capital, or that cultural capital is contextually valued.

If no clearly defined singular high-status culture exists but instead numerous signals associated with status as I argue is the case in the United States, then it is difficult to measure exactly how privilege is perpetuated in education using the cultural capital framework, particularly that linked with high-status culture (also see Peterson and Kern, 1996).

Part of the problem initiates with the French system of education that Bourdieu was studying. This system was much less accessible, open, or meritocratic than the American system (also see Turner, 1960). Tracks in primary and secondary schooling were generally not permeable but greatly influenced one's life chances. Comparatively, in the United States, education is more accessible (despite the admitted issues of variation in institutional selectivity, academic preparation, and financial barriers, among others). Although many between- and in-school inequalities exist, the system at least has the potential for flexibility (many primary or secondary school tracks aim to be permeable, flexible, and not prescriptive, for example). In sum, without accounting for these differences in educational approach, the application of Bourdieu's theory to the "open" educational system of the United States is less compelling.

Given the blurring boundaries of class in the American context, one begins to wonder what class means in such a place. Contemplating this question, Musoba and Baez (2009) argued that the term *class* in the United States cannot stand for such simplistic categories. "The class at issue in the United States, and in other heterogeneous countries—and we would guess even in France itself—cannot stand for a coherent ontological category. A class here is a matter of perspective and definition. Thus, a class can signify not only socioeconomic categories, but also racial, ethnic, linguistic, and even sexual ones" (p. 177). Perhaps including multiple categories in the notion of "class" was actually Bourdieu's aim. But without explicitly discussing other categories, the silence in much of Bourdieu's work relative to race, language, sexual orientation, or other categories implies that class equates only to socioeconomic status.

I am not asserting that privilege is not perpetuated in or through educational institutions in the United States. A significant body of evidence indicates that U.S. educational institutions contain grave inequalities (Blau, 2004; Lareau, 2003; Lee and Burkam, 2002; Winkle-Wagner, 2009b). What I am questioning here is *how* inequality is perpetuated. In some countries—perhaps in the French context that served as the lifeblood of Bourdieu's analysis—stratification is primarily class based. The United States has seen a long history of racial stratification that is often more salient than class strata, for example. Although racial inequality certainly can be and has been linked to class stratification (see Shapiro, 2004, for example), these categories are quite different in their foundations and in their manifestations.

In the U.S. context, class, race, gender, and arguably religion all may provide cultural contexts used to classify, categorize, and stratify students in educational institutions. Many times these categories are intersecting, and it can be difficult if not impossible to study the common cultural context of one without the other (one cannot study class without also looking at racial and gender-based stratification). Bourdieu's theory of cultural capital implies a dominant-subordinate dichotomy: a dominant class has a particular, common culture, and a subordinate class has a different common culture (also see Lamont and Lareau, 1988). Yet the United States has many subgroups and many dominant and subordinate cultures. The pluralism and intersection of stratifying categories in the American context makes the class-based focus of cultural capital problematic. But do class categories, at least those associated with socioeconomic status, manifest in the same way as race or gender categories as Bourdieu's silence on the subject might suggest? I am not convinced that they do.

The Absence of Race and Gender
Bourdieu did not overtly refer to race. Although he mentioned gender disparities or the different ways that men or women may appropriate cultural capital in some instances, gender is generally also absent from his substantive analyses and theoretical arguments. Gender and racial stratification were explicitly not considered in Bourdieu's *Distinction* (1979a/1984) because the participants were homogeneous in other ways, or at least it was the implicit assumption of the work. Thus, using cultural capital to analyze racial or gender categories is inconsistent with the theory unless the theoretical work is done to broaden the theory. Cultural capital has been applied to an exploration of socioeconomic inequalities in the United States to better understand the relationships between social class distinctions and educational opportunities (Lareau, 1987, 2000, 2003). Yet socioeconomic issues often intersect with race and gender in the

United States (Oliver and Shapiro, 1997; Shapiro, 2004), and cultural capital does not adequately consider this intersection, at least in its current theoretical formulation.

Despite what I consider to be a serious flaw in Bourdieu's original depiction of the reproduction of social inequality, many scholars have attempted to fill this gap by applying his ideas to racial inequality in education (see, for example, Freeman, 1997; Horvat, 2003; Kalmijn and Kraaykamp, 1996; Lareau and Horvat, 1999; Perna, 2000; Roscigno and Ainsworth-Darnell, 1999). Notwithstanding these efforts, most advances *include* race and gender as categories of inquiry or variables while still maintaining the general tenor of Bourdieu's origin of cultural capital, which includes a treatment of class-based inequality, an economic metaphor, and the potential for a deficiency approach, as I suggest below.

Extending beyond work that includes race as one of many variables or categories of analysis, some scholars have initiated notions of cultural capital that are targeted toward marginalized populations (Franklin, 2002; Yosso, 2005). In most cases, this effort is ultimately an attempt to move beyond a dominant-centered cultural capital, underlining the cultural capital that people of color have had amid historical oppression. This shift in attention from the dominant cultural capital in a social setting to an examination of that cultural capital that is marginalized or underacknowledged may breathe new life into Bourdieu's theoretical apparatus.

Yosso's (2005) work in theorizing an alternative to cultural capital (the previously mentioned community cultural wealth) comes closer to a theoretical redevelopment of cultural capital in order to apply it to racialized experiences. Through her work blending Critical Race Theory and its antecedents and subsequent adaptations, feminist theory, and specific racial or ethnic perspectives, Yosso persuasively argues for an interpretation that includes the cultural knowledge, skills, abilities, and contacts that socially marginalized groups possess that often go unrecognized. In another example, Carter (2003) crafts a notion of "Black" cultural capital of African American youth that proposes a way for marginalized populations to navigate multiple spaces.

Bourdieu might argue that the notion of habitus incorporates race more plainly. As Horvat (2001) noted, "The habitus is generated by the social conditions of lived experience, including race, ethnicity, geographical location, and gender" (p. 207). Following this logic, "race and ethnicity can be thought of as markers of class distinction" (p. 207).

Presenting a theoretical treatment of Bourdieu's framework, particularly his notion of habitus, as it relates to race, Horvat (2003) maintained that the use of habitus allows for a treatment of race and class categories simultaneously. She asserted that through the use of habitus, "we can uncover the subconscious, internalized sense of accessibility to educational opportunity for individuals. We can also provide a more accurate picture of the way in which race and class function in differing contexts across time" (p. 19).

Dumais (2002) is one of the few scholars to draw attention to the applicability of Bourdieu's theoretical structure to gendered analysis. She maintained that the idea of field might be an area where Bourdieu allowed for gendered analysis. Explicitly, different uses of cultural capital imply that social actions may take place in different fields for men and women. Habitus is also gendered in that men and women may experience different sets of available possibilities based on their sex. But most scholars who include gender include it as only one of many variables in a study rather than as a focal point of the analysis. Much more work is needed to expand the notions of field, cultural capital, habitus, and social capital in a way that centrally accounts for gendered differences in social and educational inequalities.

Attempts to study racial or gender inequality would be more convincing if the class-based aim of the initial theory were reconsidered. Class categories cannot be evenly and universally applied to race and gender categories. People in a particular racialized group or of a particular sex are not of a universal class category. The nuances, particularly as they connect with class, make the inclusion of race and gender in a cultural capital framework difficult at best.

One of the problems with cultural capital as it relates to race and gender is the acquisition of privilege. Although class-based privileges *can* be acquired through particular experiences or social networks, race and gender do not work as acquisitions in the same manner (also see Winkle-Wagner, 2009a, 2009b). For example, if one is born Black in the United States, one cannot simply acquire particular experiences or social networks to alter one's racial category in the same way that one could acquire experiences to alter the appearance of one's class categorization. Rather, race, at least in its initial ascription (that is, as one is categorized racially at birth), is ascribed in such a way as to deny agency or choice. Gender is similar in that one is ascribed a particular sex (female or male) at birth. Although one can act in gendered ways (feminine or masculine) that are unusual or outside the socially recognized norms of one's sex, the person may ultimately be sanctioned for it (perhaps excluded in some social situations). Hence, one could certainly acquire a tool kit of behaviors, ways of thinking, or speech patterns that would potentially work similarly to cultural capital (for example, Carter's, 2003 "'Black' Cultural Capital"). But it still does not explain the way that racial categories—and gender categories, for that matter—cannot be exchanged or acquired in the way that class categories can.

Eventually, the lack of attention to race and gender in the initial theoretical edifice may affect the way that cultural capital is applied and interpreted. As I argue below, the absence of race and gender awareness in the initial theorizing of cultural capital could lead, through the exclusion of nondominant peoples and perspectives, to a deficiency approach in the application of cultural capital in educational research.

A Theory of Domination and Deficiency Applications

Often drawn to the notion of cultural capital because of an interest in solving or at least understanding educational inequality, scholars have used cultural capital to study such important topics as how family background (parenting styles, investments in education) can affect educational success (Cheadle, 2008; Lareau, 2003), the way that knowledge of particular cultural norms is rewarded in schools or by institutions of higher education (Pascarella, Pierson, Wolniak, and Terenzini, 2004), the way that some schools or institutions transfer privilege to their students (Cookson and Persell, 1985), the effect of often tacit cultural knowledge or involvement on educational attainment (DiMaggio and Mohr, 1985; Roscigno and Ainsworth-Darnell, 1999), and college access (Freeman, 1997; Perna, 2000; Perna and Titus, 2005; St. John, 2006).

Despite the intention of many scholars to unmask and even solve educational inequality, Bourdieu's theory is for all intents and purposes a "theory of domination" rather than a "theory of salvation" (Musoba and Baez, 2009, p. 175). With roots in a Marxist dominant-subordinate dichotomy, Bourdieu's theoretical approach attempts to explain the way that some groups are continually subordinated to others. The attention he gives to the perpetuation of domination is one of the merits of his work. But it is the theory of domination that may ultimately keep this theory, in its current form, from becoming the type of theory that explains revolution and significant change of the social order.

Although I agree that Bourdieu went a long way toward bridging the agency-structure divide, empowering a space for human agency to begin to interact with the unequal social arrangement, the dominant-subordinate aspects of Bourdieu's theory may overshadow the potential for the type of agency that would initiate significant social change. For instance, Bourdieu's *Distinction: A Social Critique of the Judgment of Taste* (1979a/1984) includes a lengthy section with empirical evidence suggesting that the *petite bourgeoisie* (middle class) will not ultimately change its station in the social structure because of established sets of tastes and preferences (habitus). In the end, it is these long-developed sets of tastes that may discourage one from acting in a way that would be associated with a higher social status. Even if one gains upward economic mobility, his or her tastes in food or recreational activities, for example, will in many ways work to keep him or her from gaining upward mobility. Take the example of free time. Bourdieu maintained that someone who has recently gained economic mobility may still have the mind-set that she must work very hard to make ends meet and that this "hard work" ethic will keep her from taking the luxurious vacations that she could now afford. Or a person continues to crave the food that would have fueled him for manual labor (high-fat, cheap meals), even though he no longer does this type of work. These apparent "choices" are really connected more to one's earlier cultural capital and habitus than to one's current economic status, and it is, according to Bourdieu, exactly these "decisions" that will keep a person from becoming a full member of a new status group. Thus, this continuous conflict eventually goes further in explaining continued domination than it does in explaining a way out or the possibility of salvation and transformation.

It is the centrality of domination that, in applications of the theory to educational contexts, may keep Bourdieu's cultural capital (and full theoretical framework) from fully explaining some of these issues where marginalized populations attempt to make social progress such as access, achievement, or success in college (also see Musoba and Baez, 2009). That is, the end point of Bourdieu's theory applied to educational research may eventually lead to an important and vivid explanation of how marginalized populations continue to remain underserved, underrepresented, and generally disadvantaged. It is what I mean by the potential for a deficiency approach. In my view, Bourdieu's cultural capital does not readily lend itself to *altering* the domination. And it does not mean that I do not advocate the use of Bourdieu's theory. I consider Bourdieu's work to be ground-breaking in uncovering the way that domination is *perpetuated*. Rather, I am asserting that before using it, scholars, practitioners, and theorists should contemplate the implicit assumptions and potentialities of the theory itself.

The notion of meritocracy, a hallmark of advanced industrial societies like the United States, also points to a theory of domination, and when cultural capital is used in meritocratic systems of education, an even greater likelihood exists that cultural capital will explain domination rather than revolution. Meritocracy, the idea that one is rewarded on the basis of merit, ability, or achievement, is an implicit bread-and-butter kind of belief that permeates American ideology, aspirations, and expectations. The sensibility is that if one works hard, he or she will be rewarded for this work (also see Turner's, 1960, "Sponsored and Contest Mobility" argument). It is certainly the viewpoint that permeates educational institutions in the United States.

Applying meritocratic notions to cultural capital implies a "bootstrap" mentality, where one is encouraged to simply acquire more cultural capital by working harder. Like physical capital (money), cultural capital can be acquired through one's social origin (inherited wealth) or through education (acquired wealth). But the problem with this approach is that the rules for the acquisition of cultural capital are much less transparent and straightforward. In my view, Bourdieu was suspicious of the idea of a meritocracy, opting instead for a belief in the *myth* of meritocracy, that this notion would serve the status conflicts in society, reinforcing existing social stratification. Yet in the American context, Bourdieu's cultural capital has been interpreted in such a way as to *reinforce meritocratic sensibilities*. Thus, if one does not have cultural capital that is valued in an educational setting, for example, one should work harder to get it. Much of the literature directed toward acquisition of dominant cultural capital (whether it is defined as highbrow or contextually valued) implies this work ethic. Two assumptions need to be disentangled here: one is that the dominant or "valued" cultural capital is the kind of cultural capital that everyone should attempt to acquire, and the other is that it assumes that at some level everyone has equal access to cultural capital.

Cultural capital is typically measured and interpreted in the educational research literature from the dominant group's perspective, which, perhaps unwittingly, calibrates "normal" as the dominant, often the high-status, cultural capital. On the other hand, the "abnormal" (those who do not necessarily associate with high-status groups or high-status capital) becomes deficient, even if unwittingly on the part of those scholars identifying the dominant cultural capital. A common interpretation of cultural capital maintains that it is the property of the elite, not a commodity that is accessible to everyone, the highbrow cultural capital definition (Kingston, 2001; Lamont and Lareau, 1988; Lareau and Weininger, 2003). The central consideration in this approach is *not* those who are subordinated, dominated, or "minoritized" (Gilbourn, 2005), which means essentially (even if unwittingly) that if someone is "deficient" in high-status cultural capital, that person must not be working hard enough to acquire it. Although the contextually-valued cultural capital interpretation softens this sense of deficiency, an assumption still exists within this interpretation that one is "lacking" the cultural capital valued in that context, which often still conveys a sense of deficiency. But what this focus on the dominant cultural capital fails to explain is the reality that the social stratification will foster opportunities for more highbrow cultural capital acquisition for those who are already in a highbrow position (or likewise for contextually-valued cultural capital).

Linking this theory with meritocratic sensibilities, many studies contain an unstated, and possibly even unintentional, assumption that those lacking (deficient) in cultural capital could be taught it, which would solve the problem of inequality (Collier and Morgan, 2008; Pascarella et al., 2004; Tierney, 1999). This view could place the responsibility of change on the shoulders of individual students rather than pointing to unequal social structures. It also does not account for the cultural capital some have acquired from their social backgrounds (families, communities) that may provide privileges to some upon entry to educational institutions. Using a deficiency explanation, research on formal education (primary, secondary, and higher education) often begins from the assumption of helping so-called "disadvantaged" or "at-risk" students whose race or class background (often implicating one's family as deficient as well) result in their lacking the requisite knowledge, social skills, or cultural capital. Schooling or education would attempt to compensate for the lack of cultural capital that some students have failed to acquire from their families (also see García and Guerra, 2004, or Valenzuela, 1999, for discussions of deficiency approaches to education).

Applying this approach to higher education's predominantly White institutions, the implication would be to encourage students to change themselves to associate with campus mainstream (usually White and middle class at predominantly White institutions) tastes, norms, or values. Ultimately, if applied in this way, cultural capital applications and interpretations could be hegemonic, celebrating some cultural ways of knowing over others. This argument is the primary one of many scholars who ponder cultural capital as it relates (or fails to relate) to people of color or other historically marginalized groups (see Franklin, 2002; Yosso, 2005). Theories primarily center on minoritized students (the way that poor or working-class students are educated) and could at least be useful in helping to explain the gaps in many of the cultural capital interpretations that only consider dominant groups. Ultimately, Bourdieu's focal point of explaining the cultural capital of majority groups (the dominant) adapted in most educational research (and in Bourdieu's empirical work, too) could lead to a deficiency approach. The resulting assumption is that "some communities are culturally wealthy while others are culturally poor. This interpretation of Bourdieu exposes White middle-class culture as the standard and therefore all other forms and expressions of 'culture' are judged in comparison to this 'norm'" (Yosso, 2005, p. 76). Clearly, more work is needed to refocus cultural capital in a way that is not primarily associated with dominant groups, but it may take significant theorizing to reinterpret cultural capital in a nondominant way so that it does not simply reinforce the theory of domination underlying meritocracy.

Methodological Limitations of Cultural Capital Applications

In addition to substantive limitations, methodological limitations affect the way that cultural capital has been interpreted and applied in educational research: the operationalization of cultural capital in empirical research, and the absence of the full theory in empirical work.

The Definition and Operationalization of Cultural Capital in Research

Perhaps the greatest methodological problem identified by Lamont and Lareau (1988) and later by Kingston (2001) is in the definition or operationalization of the concept in research processes. Although cultural capital is defined or theoretically explained in four primary ways in educational research (highbrow, contextually-valued, otherized, and in a Bourdieuian framework), the way that cultural capital is actually operationalized—that is, defined through variables in quantitative work or data linked to the theoretical notion in qualitative work—varies significantly.

The vast majority of quantitative studies have used the "holy trinity" of variables as proxies for cultural capital: parents' educational attainment level, parents' occupation, and family income. The assumption is that the higher the parents' education, occupation, and income, the more likely it is that a student will have access to the highbrow cultural capital or to the cultural capital that is valued in a particular school or educational setting. Some studies add parents' educational expectations or language spoken in the home to this trifecta (for example, Perna and Titus, 2005). Similarly, the assumption is that if the common language (English) is spoken in the home or if parents have higher expectations of their children, then these children are more likely to have access to cultural capital that can be appropriated in education. In many quantitative studies, the variables are primarily classified as dummy variables, and the student is labeled as having cultural capital or lacking it (also see Noble and Davies, 2009).

The reason for the common use of these variables is mainly a data issue, as they really may be the most appropriate markers of cultural capital in a particular dataset. One of the most important limits of this particular operationalization of cultural capital is the distinct possibility for a disparity among family education, income, and occupation and actual activities or involvement of children relative to the acquisition of cultural capital. This issue is one Coleman (1988) addressed in his consideration of social capital. Although my concentration is not on social capital, part of Coleman's argument is relevant here: it is possible for parents to be highly educated, have a high-status occupation, and have a high income but for their children not to reap the benefits in terms of cultural capital. In my estimation, Coleman (1988) was unreasonably biased against women working outside the home in his discussion (he implied that children who lacked social capital often lacked it because their mother worked outside the home); his point was that parents and children may not actually interact that much, particularly in higher-status families. The crux of this argument is important—that family education, income, and occupation may not be a good proxy for the acquisition of cultural capital, particularly in the absence of other markers.

More recently, quantitative studies have started to operationalize cultural capital in more nuanced ways. Variables used as proxies for cultural capital have begun to include measurements for cultural classes taken by students, students' cultural activities (visits to museums or theaters), or culturally relevant objects in the home (books, artwork, computers, for example). These variables suggest a more dynamic empirical study of cultural capital because they allow for a possible comparison between background variables (family income, education, and occupation) with students' actual activities relative to the acquisition of culturally relevant knowledge, skills, or abilities (see Cheadle, 2008; Perna and Titus, 2005).

Quantitative scholars are not the only ones who must be held culpable for the multitude of definitions of cultural capital; cultural capital has been applied to qualitative work in a variety of ways. Cultural capital has been characterized as everything from the way families structure their children's free time (Lareau, 2003) to part of what creates an "organizational habitus" that privileges particular groups of students over others (McDonough, 1997) to cultural knowledge (Freeman, 1997) that could be used to navigate peer groups (Carter, 2003). Certainly, the qualitative interpretations of cultural capital are generally more nuanced. They often do allow for the potential discrepancies in what might seem to be obvious markers of a family's status and the way that students may or may not be able to appropriate cultural capital.

One of the more salient tribulations in the qualitative work is that it is often not clear how researchers analyze their work related to their theoretical idea of cultural capital. Are scholars looking for particular markers of the acquisition or appropriation of culturally related knowledge, skills, or competencies and then coding the qualitative data as "cultural capital"? If so, what are these markers? Or are researchers allowing themes or categories to emerge from the data, as is frequently suggested in qualitative methodologies (Carspecken, 1996; Creswell, 1998; Denzin and Lincoln, 2003), and then reflecting on cultural capital amid these emerging themes and interpretations? Or do scholars begin qualitative work without a theoretical framework in mind and then find a connection with cultural capital (the approach suggested by grounded theory, as in Charmaz, 2005; Denzin and Lincoln, 2003)? Bourdieu's work would suggest an iterative process, a back-and-forth movement, between data analysis and reflection on theory. But aside from a few notable exceptions, much of the qualitative scholarship does not actually indicate how, beyond a general discussion in a section on the theoretical framework, cultural capital actually comes into the analysis and interpretation of the data.

As Lamont and Lareau (1988) argued, "This proliferation of definitions, undoubtedly a sign of intellectual vitality—and possibly, of the fruitfulness of the concept—has created sheer confusion. We are now reaching a point where cultural capital could become obsolete" (p. 153). Twenty years later, even more definitions have been used for "cultural capital," and the confusion continues.

The Absence of the Full Theory in Empirical Work

The majority of the empirical studies that aim to identify the acquisition or appropriation of cultural capital in educational settings do not employ the full theoretical model as Bourdieu may have intended. Of the studies reviewed in the previous chapter, approximately only one in three referred to field, habitus, or social capital (thirty-nine out of 105 or 37 percent). I grouped studies into the Bourdieuian framework category if they mentioned habitus, field, *or* social capital—a generous categorization in that Bourdieu's full framework would really require the use of field and habitus in particular (also see Horvat, 2003). This gap is like trying to enjoy a cake by eating eggs, sugar, and flour separately; these ingredients simply are not representative of a cake until they are mixed and baked together. Cultural capital is essentially meaningless without mentioning or examining the field in which it is contextualized. The field is what blends together the meaning and the system of rewards or sanctions based on one's cultural background. Bourdieu (1979a/1984) maintains that the field is the "marketplace" that gives cultural capital its value and meaning. Habitus is important in that it alludes to the range of potential actions that one might perceive as available (the set of dispositions, tastes, or preferences).

Many of those studies that explore cultural capital and social capital together conflate these concepts as if they are unmasking the same processes (for example, Saunders and Serna, 2004; Wells, 2008). These studies often do not distinguish variables for cultural or social capital, simply using one set of variables as proxies for both. In qualitative work, the interpretations talk about how a particular aspect of data suggests "cultural and social capital" but do not identify the differences between them. This approach is problematic just as is the use of family education, occupation, and income as markers for cultural capital: social and cultural capital are related, but they identify different aspects of cultural and social privilege. To be precise, cultural capital refers to cultural skills, knowledge, competencies, or abilities, while social capital refers to relationships and interactions. Certainly, cultural capital could not be appropriated without relationships. But the actual capital of human relationships (social capital) differs from cultural capital (degrees, cultural involvement, knowledge of particular music, dress, food, etc.). Thus, these distinct theoretical constructs should be disentangled in research because one could potentially have a great deal of cultural capital valued in a particular field but not have the social capital to be able to appropriate it. Or one could possess plenty of social capital but not have the cultural capital to be able to use it. Nuances are overlooked in conflating these theoretical ideas.

Conclusion

Although I am admittedly not an avid bowler, the metaphor of bowling may apply here to my analysis of the strengths and limitations in the use of cultural capital in educational research. Cultural capital, and those applying and interpreting it in educational research, have rolled "strikes" in many ways: the expansion of capital theories to include less tangible perpetuators of privilege, the bridging of the agency-structure gap, and the implications for methodology from Bourdieu's work, including the link between theory and data and macro- and microlevels of research. All of these "strikes" suggest that the use of cultural capital and the theory of social reproduction in which it is included hold great promise. Yet all things considered, some significant "gutter balls" must be identified before tallying the final score. First, the use of an economic metaphor to describe cultural capital has limitations. Second, cultural capital is often considered peripheral in the way that moral boundaries may influence inclusionary and exclusionary processes or the way that people associate others as part of their group. The assumption of homogenous class-based privilege in Bourdieu's theoretical apparatus may not apply to a pluralistic, American (or similar), context. Importantly, the centrality of class-based analysis may disregard race and gender, even while these categories may play a large role in social reproduction processes. This factor, along with the emphasis on domination rather than revolution, may imply a deficiency approach, blaming those who lack the cultural capital that is valued in a particular setting for their insufficiencies. Finally, relative to methodology, the lack of consistent definitions and interpretations of cultural capital in the research is problematic, potentially resulting in a concept that has lost its meaning. Hope exists that placing cultural capital in the full theory of social reproduction that Bourdieu advanced may help to remedy this issue. All told, it is not just how one releases the ball that matters in bowling or in the use of cultural capital in educational research. Rather, the approach to releasing the ball at the foul line may significantly influence the player's outcomes. Likewise, a scholar's understanding of the origins, assumptions, and intentions of cultural capital may dramatically influence the outcomes of his or her research.

Revolutionary Possibilities?
The Future of Cultural Capital
in Educational Research

IT SEEMS APPROPRIATE to end this monograph about the study of cultural capital in educational settings as I began it—with another example of a discussion of the concept with my students. I began with an example from one of my classes in which graduate students seemed to know of cultural capital without fully understanding its meaning or background. In my graduate-level sociology of education course, where the concept of cultural capital is one of the key theoretical learning objectives in the class, one of my students inquired recently, "But how can we stop some forms of cultural capital from being valued so highly in education over others? How can we make the cultural capital that is not dominant more accepted by the mainstream?" With my student's question in mind, I ask, Is it possible to facilitate a "symbolic revolution that questions the very foundations of the production and reproduction of symbolic capital" (Bourdieu and Wacquant, 1992, p. 174)? Even if a full revolution of the valuing of cultural capital does not occur, what might be the future of this theoretical construct, particularly in educational research? Although methodological and substantive pitfalls certainly have occurred in the interpretation and application of cultural capital, the potential of the concept to explain the transmission of power and privilege still imparts too much promise for me to recommend not using it in research. This final chapter considers ways that cultural capital could be revised or expanded theoretically and ideas for the future use of this concept in empirical research. It concludes with some implications of cultural capital research for educational practice.

Theoretical Considerations

Theoretical advancement relative to cultural capital and Bourdieu's larger theory of social reproduction has rich potential. This theoretical progress could include concerns about the definition of cultural capital, the use of Bourdieu's full theoretical equipment, race and gender categories relative to cultural capital, and the transferability of cultural capital to different country contexts.

Cultural Capital Definitions

As argued in this monograph, one of the primary problems with the current body of educational research that uses cultural capital is the operationalization or definition of the concept. Cultural capital was defined in four common ways in the research reviewed here: as cultural knowledge or competence linked to highbrow elite status; as those cultural competencies, skills, or abilities valued in a particular context; as part of a Bourdieuian framework that aims to uncover the transmission of power and privilege; and as those cultural skills, abilities, knowledge, or competencies of nondominant groups.

A few scholars have identified this issue of operationalization or definition, and noteworthy attempts have been made to propose definitions that could be more universally used. For example, Lamont and Lareau (1988) endeavored to identify a common definition that might be applicable across educational studies, noting that "cultural capital is institutionalized, i.e., widely shared, high-status cultural signals (attitudes, preferences, formal knowledge, behaviors, goals, and credentials) used for social and cultural exclusion" (p. 156). Lamont and Lareau's definition would allow for the acquisition of cultural capital through one's social origin or through education. This definition, consistent with Bourdieu's (1979a/1984) empirical focus on the transmission of high-status culture, centers on the institutional type of cultural capital, disregarding cultural capital that is embodied (one's sense of culture, traditions, norms) or objectified (things that one owns). Given that most educational researchers and practitioners are likely to be more centered on the way in which those in educational settings reward, sanction, create, or maintain cultural capital, perhaps emphasizing the institutional type of cultural capital is appropriate. But certainly ways exist in which embodied or objectified cultural capital might be studied in educational settings, and the research might be remiss if it focused only on institutionalized cultural capital, particularly, as I argued in the previous chapter, as much of the educationally rewarded cultural capital is now in the embodied form. Additionally, some scholars have criticized this definition as overly reliant on high-brow culture, although it was not the authors' intent (Lareau and Weininger, 2003).

Theoretical labor is needed relative to cultural capital that allows for the microlevel interactions that work to create, reify, or reward particular types of cultural capital in a given field. As a charge to educational scholars and theorists, Lareau and Weininger (2003) argued that a "broader conception [is needed] that stresses the microinteractional processes through which individuals comply (or fail to comply) with the evaluative standards of dominant institutions such as schools" (p. 568). By "microinteractional processes," these scholars mean the direct or indirect "imposition of evaluative norms favoring the children or families of a particular social milieu" need to be examined (p. 568). This interpretation allows a meaningful consideration of both dominant and nondominant forms of cultural capital to be explored. It is clear, however, that more theoretical analysis is needed to craft clear and consistent definitions that can be used broadly by educational researchers and practitioners.

All told, after reviewing the studies for this monograph, I promote the use of cultural capital in Bourdieu's full theoretical scheme because it submits the clearest statement of the interaction between an individual and the social structure. Bourdieu's framework, including the concepts of field and habitus, suggests the contextually-valued interpretation of cultural capital and then better enables an explanation of the context in which cultural capital is valued. Using the contextually-valued definition of cultural capital in the full theoretical scaffolding bolsters the explanatory potential of the concept. That said, the definition of cultural capital in educational research studies must be clearer, both in the theoretical discussion or framework and in empirical applications (what variables or data are used as proxies for cultural capital).

Bourdieu's Theory of Social Reproduction

Horvat (2001) called for more "Bourdieuian research" in higher education that incorporates Bourdieu's full theoretical apparatus as a way to uncover social inequality, proffering suggestions for ways that this research could be structured (pp. 215–216). Yet currently the vast majority of educational research studies that employ cultural capital for primary, secondary, and post-secondary education do so using cultural capital in absence of the larger theory of which it is a part. This failure to consider Bourdieu's full theory of social reproduction (outlined in the first chapter) is problematic because cultural capital is highly dependent on the other concepts, the notion of field in particular. Cultural capital is relevant only in the field, or marketplace, in which it is recognized and given its value. Bourdieu would maintain that outside a particular field (a family unit, a school, a community, and so on), cultural capital may hold no value, rendering it essentially meaningless, at least for the transmission of status and privilege. Additionally, the concept of habitus is important for an accurate use of the cultural capital concept. One's habitus—one's set of dispositions, tastes, and preferences—basically determines the available set of options that seems viable for appropriating cultural capital, implying that even if one did possess the cultural capital that was highly valued in a particular setting but did not have the habitus to understand how to appropriate this cultural capital for oneself or how to turn that capital into something meaningful, the cultural capital would again be rendered effectively worthless.

Swartz (1997) enumerated recommendations for the necessary steps to conduct research in a manner incorporating Bourdieu's full theoretical edifice, maintaining that the research must:

Specify what is under investigation and relate it to the broader field of power.

Identify the positions of all the actors in the field of study, their relationships to one another, and their access to and control over the valued capital (cultural capital) in that field.

Examine the habitus brought by actors to their respective positions along with the social trajectory that these actors pursue in the larger field of struggle.

These recommendations could pertain to either qualitative or quantitative work. It is a tall order from Swartz, particularly for quantitative scholarship, given that many researchers are constrained by the datasets they use. Yet future research must at least consider these issues so as not to divorce cultural capital from its meaning in a larger theory of social reproduction. Even if the available data do not fully explain habitus, for example, a researcher should at least mention it as a potential limitation of the study. But regardless of one's dataset, it is imperative that the field—the social setting that the data are attempting to analyze—be well defined because it is the marketplace that gives cultural capital its value and ultimately its meaning.

The use of Bourdieu's full theoretical structure in qualitative research implies that the research, located in the microlevel interpretations of everyday lived experiences, should be linked to the larger social structure in which it occurs. Although some critical research methodologies maintain that this criterion is not only possible but vital to making qualitative research explanatory of oppressive forces (Carspecken, 1996), a large body of qualitative work misses this opportunity entirely.

With this caveat in mind, I will give an example of how it might be achieved, using critical qualitative methodology (also see Winkle-Wagner, 2009a, 2009b). In his critical ethnographic methodology and critical epistemology (that is, way of knowing, how one knows that one knows), Carspecken (1996) calls for qualitative research to eventually endeavor to conduct "system level" analysis—a way of collecting the appropriate data that might shed light on the larger social structures and processes in which the participants' experiences are located. Yet even if one does not achieve this point in the research process, Carspecken still roots his analytical framework in the larger social structure. Doing so entails a rigorous consideration of the data that a researcher analyzes in qualitative work, delving deeper into the meaning in and behind participants' statements and actions to understand how these statements or actions might represent larger social processes and inequalities. To do so means contemplating current and historical inequalities in the larger social structure and the way that these inequalities might influence participants' experiences. It is an iterative, reflective, sometimes messy, and imperfect process. But it also adds rigor to the process. Although qualitative work is generally not conducted for the purpose of larger generalizations, this type of social structural analysis or thinking makes qualitative work potentially more relevant to revealing, from the analysis of interactions and microlevel information, insight into the larger social structures. This example is only one; scholars should identify, create, and use others as well.

Applying cultural capital to qualitative work requires that one define the field of study and inquire into a participant's cultural knowledge, competencies, skills, or abilities. Qualitative observations could elucidate aspects of a participant's habitus and the way a participant does or does not appropriate cultural capital. Researchers need to think carefully about how questions asked of participants relate to uncovering cultural capital. Then scholars should carefully explain the way that the data analysis process connected with cultural capital. For instance, did the researcher devise categories or themes relevant to cultural capital before coding or analyzing data? Or did the research allow themes, categories, or claims to emerge through analysis before the connection with cultural capital could be contemplated? Regardless of the approach, the data analysis must be more clearly explicated and connected with the theoretical framework of which cultural capital is a part.

Last, more work is needed to identify ways to better use the Bourdieuian framework to understand the cultural capital of those who are typically not in the position to produce or place the value on it. Some theoretical reasoning spotlights nondominant cultural capital (Carter, 2003), the cultural capital those in marginalized or historically oppressed groups possess. This line of work is not inconsistent with Bourdieu; he did identify dominant and nondominant cultural capital in his reasoning. But in the main, relatively little work gives central consideration to nondominant cultural capital (thirteen of 105 studies here or 12 percent). Yet I argue that, for cultural capital to be revolutionized in the way that the quote above from Bourdieu suggests, more attention must be given to the cultural capital of nondominant groups. For new forms of cultural capital to be relevant and valued in a particular field, the nondominant forms of cultural capital must be understood and highlighted. One step in this direction would be to incorporate discussions of race or gender more centrally in cultural capital studies and frameworks.

Race, Gender, and Cultural Capital
Relatively few scholars, in my view, have attempted to do the theoretical development necessary to adequately capture cultural capital as it relates to concepts

such as race and gender. Bourdieu did not disentangle race, gender, and class categories. Rather, he implied that "class" was a categorical marker that could be inclusive of categories like race or gender. But his empirical work and consequently the tenor of his theoretical stance were largely *not* directed toward race and gender but rather concentrated on socioeconomic status. My concern, as I described in the previous chapter, is that in a racialized society like the United States (and arguably France in many ways as well), multiple aspects of oppression may be manifested in different ways. Given that only 12 percent of the studies reviewed here highlighted nondominant cultural capital, a theoretical consideration of race and gender as they do (or perhaps do not) relate to cultural capital is ripe for study.

One way to begin this work might be to shift conceptions of cultural capital away from spotlighting the privilege of dominant or historically privileged groups toward considerations of underprivileged, "subcultural" (Bullen and Kenway, 2005) or "minoritized" (Gilbourn, 2005) groups. Yosso (2005) presented an example of one such theoretical analysis in her notion of "community cultural wealth," attempting to shift from a focal point of White upper-class people toward an examination of the capital of communities of color. Her work aims at learning from the cultural knowledge, skills, abilities, and contact of those in marginalized groups. This scholarship portrays an important extension of Bourdieu's scholarship, one that I believe would be amenable to Bourdieu's intentions because it allows for the revelation of the other side of cultural capital acquisition and appropriation. But another important difference in the otherized notions of cultural capital is that they are typically more communal than Bourdieu's initial theorizing would suggest. Franklin (2002) put forth a communal interpretation of cultural capital as "the sense of group consciousness and collective identity that serves as a resource aimed at the advancement of an entire group" (p. 177). It is implicitly assumed that cultural capital, in Bourdieu's initial crafting of the concept, ultimately is possessed by the individual, although some communities certainly would have greater access to high-status cultural capital than others. Thus, the newer innovations should underscore the point that they are deliberately more communal interpretations of cultural capital, differentiated from the individualism implied by Bourdieu's work.

Gendered theorizing has been ignored by the bulk of the studies to date, aside from including gender as a variable in some studies. But in my view, a serious scrutiny of the gendered ways that cultural capital acquisition and appropriation is likely manifested remains to be done. This gap affords a rich area for future study.

Taken together, there might be a few ways that scholars could theoretically expand on the cultural capital idea to make it more applicable to race or gender stratification as it is experienced in a pluralistic society like the United States. But I would recommend a few important guidelines to at least consider before doing this important theoretical work:

Explicitly note whether the orientation of the theoretical analysis is aimed at explaining the perpetuation of high-status privilege or is geared toward an analysis of the way that power is more generally experienced by those in marginalized groups (the nondominant cultural capital).

Plainly define what is meant by the word "class." Is it meant to imply socio-economic status stratifications, or is "class" a marker of a group of people that could include race or gender classifications? These issues must be unambiguously explained. Then, the analysis and interpretation of research must reflect these decisions in the way that variables are assigned, models are created, and analysis techniques are structured.

Identify whether the theoretical reasoning considers cultural capital as an individual or public good. In other words, if cultural capital is possessed, is it the possession of a group (Franklin's, 2002, definition) or an individual (implied in Bourdieu's, 1979b/1987, analysis)?

Include at least a brief description of the history of power related to race and gender in the United States to better describe the way that the metaphor of capital (acquisition, expenditure, revenue, and so on) does or does not relate to race or gender acquisition and appropriation. In qualitative work, ponder the way that participants describe class, race, and gender issues. Do they seem to imply differences in the way that these categories are acquired and manifested in educational settings? If so, explain how it connects to class, race, and gender categories.

Use the concepts of field and habitus to proffer a more meaningful theoretical treatment of power, privilege, and social reproduction within the analysis and interpretation of data.

With these issues in mind, it is possible for reconsiderations of cultural capital to be more adaptable to race and gender categories and to begin to remedy some of the other challenges with the applications and interpretations of the concept. For example, Olneck's (2000) examination of cultural capital in light of a multicultural education framework "recodes practices represented as 'deficiencies' as 'distinctive learning styles' and as strengths upon which to build" (p. 324). This theoretical project "validates students' experiences and 'cultural referents' as worthy of classroom study and activity" (p. 324). This concept might be a tonic to the deficiency limitation that I identified in the previous chapter. Olneck notes, "The incorporation of students' cultural repertoires reorganizes school practices in ways that dissolve dichotomies by which minority students had been classified negatively" (p. 324). It is this kind of theoretical reconceptualization that is necessary to make cultural capital more applicable to race and gender groupings in the American context, which may mean, as it did in Olneck's analysis, that cultural capital needs to be blended with other theoretical frameworks.

Country Context and Cultural Capital

Although Bourdieu's work was centered on French society, it has certainly been applied globally. As the map presented in the second chapter indicates, among the 105 studies reviewed here, there were eleven different country contexts (including the United States) where the concept was applied and interpreted relative to education. I question whether the appropriate consideration is always given to the differences in these contexts. Ultimately, Bourdieu contemplated cultural capital among a relatively homogeneous population, or at least he framed it as such. Although France is certainly diverse, the way that Bourdieu theorized and empirically tested his notions of cultural capital, habitus, field, and social capital largely assumed homogeneity relative to all categories besides class (defined primarily as socioeconomic status). And one could argue that pluralism might be more salient in a country like the United States, where many citizens immigrated from other contexts.

I appreciate Bourdieu's explanation (1979a/1984) of dominant norms and behaviors as they relate to education. He ultimately maintained that educational institutions are most often created by and for the elite, the dominant class. Those who are not in this dominant class who gain entry to these institutions must contend with the norms, values, attitudes, and behaviors that the dominant class maintains are appropriate in that setting. My own work about the college experiences of African American women (Winkle-Wagner, 2009a, 2009b), while *not* rooted in a cultural capital framework, comes to similar conclusions although emphasizing the role that racial inequality plays in perpetuating domination.

A new formulation of cultural capital that takes into account the plurality of American society is needed. Namely, cultural capital, if it focuses on class as socioeconomic status, must also account for the way that socioeconomic status has become racialized in the American context (see, for example, Conley, 1999/2010; Shapiro, 2004). It is not enough to simply say that race or gender might be a "class" grouping. The theoretical endeavor must be done to connect race, gender, and socioeconomic status. To be precise, the historical accumulation of wealth can be traced back to racist policies in the United States, which has created a long-term race-based disparity related to socioeconomic status (Conley, 1999/2010; Shapiro, 2004). If a theoretical accounting of the historical challenges in a pluralistic society were presented, in my view, cultural capital could become a much more powerful theoretical tool to capture the empirical perpetuation of inequality in U.S. educational institutions. One endeavor that moves in this direction is Lamont's (1992) boundary work comparing the cultural boundary creation and maintenance of White middle-class American and French men. Conceivably, the theoretical implications of Lamont's work could be applied to educational contexts, allowing for a more robust analysis of race and gender related to "cultural capital," although more work would need to be done to extend this boundary work relative to marginalized populations because members of racial minority groups were excluded from the final analysis in Lamont's study. But the notion of moral boundaries remains a potentially powerful connector between cultural capital and race or gender categories.

Another important distinction that needs to be made for the American country context is the *type* of cultural capital that seems to hold the most power. Partially because of the unique form of capitalism in the United States and partly because of the mass production of goods (Holt, 1998), the study of the objectified form of cultural capital (books in the home, computers, artwork, and so on) may not be the best marker of status, at least absent the measurement of other forms of cultural capital (those objectified goods combined with embodied cultural capital or institutionalized cultural capital). As Lareau's (2003) work about recreational time in families suggests, cultural capital has become more and more embodied in current times, particularly in the United States. This observation does not imply that books or computers in the home, for example, are unimportant. It is simply that these objectified goods may not be the primary marker of status in the way that they once were, largely because goods are more and more accessible to the masses. Measuring embodied cultural capital only as educational credentials also gives short shrift to the subtle ways that privilege might be perpetuated in the American context. The study of embodied cultural capital as leisure time (see, for example, Lareau, 2003) such as vacations, hobbies, social outings, sports, or recreational activities may be a better measurement of cultural capital (also see Holt, 1998).

One way to begin to better identify the country context of cultural capital is through the notion of "field." The field must be carefully defined as it relates to the country context. It may not be enough to simply delineate the "field" as a particular school, for example. Rather, the "school field" will be very different in a particular state, region, or country milieu. The school is located in a particular neighborhood, state, region, or country context, and all these overlapping layers of "field" complexity influence the "marketplace" in which cultural capital is given its meaning and value. Cultural capital and the related Bourdieuian concepts would have more explanatory muscle if the notion of "field" were to be defined in this more complex manner. Indeed, the definition of terms like this one connects theoretical and methodological possibilities.

Methodological Considerations

It is imperative that scholars using cultural capital provide a definition of the type of cultural capital (institutionalized, embodied, objectified) at the heart of their analysis. Additionally, it is essential that the definition of cultural capital not be simply assumed but explicitly defined, then the definition linked to the available data in the study. Researchers should begin to compare their intended definition of cultural capital with the available variables in their datasets in quantitative research and with the emergent themes in qualitative work. Discrepancies between the theoretically possible definitions and the use of available data should be explained. In other words, although scholars may want to use a theoretically dynamic definition, the data may or may not fit that definition; these variations should be made explicit.

Given the two-tiered acquisition of cultural capital through social origin and education, multilevel modeling will be particularly useful for quantitative studies. To offer a robust depiction of the way that cultural capital is or is not acquired and appropriated, one must simultaneously examine schools, families, and communities where students are embedded. Bourdieu maintained that cultural capital can be a cumulative advantage: those who acquire cultural capital that is valued in schools from their families or communities will be privileged in education. Multilevel modeling (see, for example, Cheadle, 2008; Núñez, 2009; Perna and Titus, 2005) begins to reveal these complexities in a way that more two-dimensional statistical models cannot.

The way that variables are defined in the models could also be more complex. In statistical models, researchers need to shift away from the use of dummy variables that imply that one either has or does not have cultural capital. For instance, Noble and Davies (2009) developed a cultural capital questionnaire that allows for more nuanced explanations of gradations of cultural capital. But it is likely that the possession of cultural capital could be better expressed on a continuum rather than framed as a zero-sum game where one either does or does not have it.

One of the challenges to the quantitative or macrolevel study of cultural capital in education is the available data. Large, national datasets that will allow for the kind of generalization that many scholars desire to make do not always allow for ideal variables that serve as appropriate proxies for cultural capital. Measurements such as the way students appropriate or "exchange" cultural capital in educational settings (that is, cultural involvement in and out of schools) are simply not always available, nor are measurements of families' actual tastes and preferences in food, clothing, and music often available. It is another reason that qualitative inquiry may be particularly effective in representing some of the necessary nuances of cultural capital acquisition and appropriation and the way that it influences educational outcomes in the American context. But it could also be a charge for the development of better datasets that would award more holistic and useful measurements that relate well to the notions of cultural capital, habitus, field, and social capital. With this caveat in mind, for instance, Nora (2004) created a survey instrument to measure constructs of cultural capital and habitus as they relate to students' college decision-making processes (also see Noble and Davies, 2009). In the end, if such datasets and instruments are developed, it would be most informative if they were longitudinal so that one could ascertain the way that a person initially acquired cultural capital and then appropriated it throughout his educational and eventually occupational career. Additionally, such a dataset should converge not only on questions that attempt to uncover cultural knowledge and competence but also on one's skills or abilities (to inquire into the way that one actually uses cultural capital for educational rewards). Such a task could be one's entire research agenda. In the meantime, for those who use the datasets that are available despite their limitations, the limits must be identified and discussed so that it is clear what is and what is not actually evidenced in the study. More work should be conducted to find exemplars of ways to operationalize the nuances of cultural capital (see, for example, Pearce and Lin, 2007).

Qualitative methodology may be particularly useful in explaining the nuances of cultural capital in the American context. One reason is that cultural capital implies a global set of behaviors, attitudes, preferences, or tastes that an individual acquires and appropriates in educational settings. Qualitative methodology, particularly ethnography, which aims at understanding culture and everyday experiences, can perhaps better evaluate the nuances of an entire environment. The global nature of the concept can be difficult, although not impossible with advanced modeling, to assess using quantitative methodology, because the underlying assumption of cultural capital is that one needs to study the educational environment in its entirety—difficult to do through variables. That is, because scholars need to create a variable for cultural capital concepts, at times the variables cannot shed light on the nuances of social reproduction and the perpetuation of privilege that the cultural capital concept may theoretically imply. This observation is not to say that cultural capital should be studied only with qualitative methodology; rather, it is a cautionary note about the need to carefully evaluate the way that variables are constructed in quantitative work to confirm that the data are actually evidence of the cultural capital.

For those who do use qualitative methodologies to inquire into the acquisition and appropriation of cultural capital in educational settings, more attention needs to be given to the way that data are analyzed in light of Bourdieu's theoretical foundation. Extending this framework through empirical work must also be explicated clearly. It must be clear whether one developed cultural capital coding schemes before analyzing data, based on Bourdieu's framework, or whether one is allowing themes, categories, and claims to emerge and then reflecting on Bourdieu's theoretical structure.

Educational Practice Applications of Cultural Capital Research

In presenting an extensive review of the way that cultural capital has been interpreted and applied in educational research over the past thirty years, I have not given considerable attention to the practical applications of the research findings. Although educational practice has not been the heart of my work here, it is not meant to imply that the potential lessons from cultural capital studies are trivial. On the contrary, amid the strengths and limitations of the research processes and findings are many substantial conclusions that can be made relative to the practical applications of cultural capital studies. Hence, I would be remiss to end this monograph without at least mentioning some ideas for applying the lessons of these studies to educational practice, because this practice is in many ways the lifeblood of the educational settings about which I have been writing. Using the Bourdieuian framework and the findings of the large corpus of research that employs this framework could offer great promise for making educational practice more equitable. Each of Bourdieu's concepts has practical implications for teachers, professors, and administrators.

The Field of Educational Practice

The concept of field could be useful for holistically examining the schooling or institutional context. Educational practitioners can inquire into the explicit and implicit structure of the environment. One way to initiate this type of assessment could be through an analysis of the various components of the educational environment. In a review of higher education environments, Strange and Banning (2001) asserted four types of environments: *physical* (the objective space including buildings and classrooms); *aggregate* (the general type of people in the environment); *organizational* (administrative structure, policies and procedures, and so on); and *constructed* (people's perceptions of the environment). These four aspects of the environment would make a good assessment of an educational "field" for K–12 or postsecondary schools. Educational practitioners could evaluate the field of schools or higher education institutions informally, or if practitioners desired to be more formalized in their evaluation of the educational field, a cultural audit (see, for example, Harper and Hurtado, 2007) might be one way to shed light on the practices and structure of the setting and how it excludes and includes particular groups of students, staff, and faculty.

After an evaluation of the various aspects of the environment or field, as I advocate researchers using Bourdieu's constructs to do, the context then needs to be reflected toward the larger social-structural environment. How does the campus or school environment reflect the environment of the community where it is located? How does the community relate to the state or region? How does the state or region relate to the larger country? Do aspects of the campus or school environment seem to reflect these larger social-structural contexts? In particular, do issues of inequality appear to be reinforced in the school or campus that are really larger social issues? This last question could of course become an entire monograph in itself, but practitioners should ask it nonetheless.

Cultural Capital in Educational Practice

Understanding the cultural capital of students and those in an educational setting more generally begins with a consideration of one's own cultural capital. Educational practitioners must conduct some self-reflection and -analysis to inquire into the cultural knowledge, competence, skills, and abilities they value. It could occur in many ways, a few examples of which follow. Reflection about one's cultural capital can begin with a simple assessment of explicit tastes or preferences: food, clothing, music, recreational activities. Then, one can continue to contemplate other culturally relevant markers that one values: language or style of speaking, behavior that one sees as "normal" or "abnormal," "rude" or "polite." Finally, one must reflect on one's own background candidly: What was the socioeconomic background of one's upbringing? What might have been the predominant socioeconomic background of one's schooling at each level? All such self-appraisals can foster an understanding of one's own valued "cultural capital."

After self-reflection, educational practitioners should begin evaluating the educational context as it may relate to the exchange and valuing of particular cultural capital. Who or what seems to be valued in the setting? Who or what seems to be devalued in the setting? The answers to these questions may be more difficult to uncover than it initially seems because answering the questions ultimately requires educational practitioners to ask themselves who and what *they* might value or devalue in the educational setting. One way to arrive at the answers might be to ask oneself, if one is a teacher or faculty member, for example: Who are the students with whom I most struggle? Which students do I most admire or enjoy? What are the characteristics of each group of students? Why might I feel this way about these different groups of students? Do others in this institution react the same to these particular groups of students? Finally, do certain groups or students appear to be continually disadvantaged in this setting? What might the cultural capital of their upbringing be, and how might it be valued (or not) in this setting? As a teacher, am I assigning homework that might be much more difficult for some students to complete (for example, an assignment that requires a particular computer software program when some students may not own a computer)? This last question, like the previous one, means beginning to talk candidly with students about their backgrounds to better understand the ways that institutions do or do not value them.

Habitus and Educational Practice

Adding to one's self-appraisal of one's cultural capital, educational practitioners can begin to identify their habitus or set of dispositions and preferences.

This identification may be one of the more difficult components of Bourdieu's framework to make tangible in educational practice. Perhaps one activity that educational practitioners could carry out is to recall their own college choice process. What colleges were on one's list of choices during this process? Where were these institutions? How many were on the list? What institutions were *not* on the list? Why? How might this list of choices relate to another person's list? Undergoing this exercise is one way to underscore the choices that might have once been personally available (or unavailable). Another exercise might be to consider the friends of one's family while growing up. Were these people similar to one's parents or guardians in educational attainment and occupational status? Did these friends have college degrees or advanced degrees? And who are one's current friends and close contacts? What characteristics do these people have in common? These last questions begin to shift toward identifying one's social capital, as explained below.

At this point, educational practitioners can begin to examine the students with whom they work. Consider the students who might seem to be most advantaged (be careful to avoid stereotypes here). How have these students discussed their future aspirations, for example? Do they seem to have a large list of options that they perceive as available to them? Next, consider the students who appear to struggle in this educational context. How do they describe their aspirations for the future?

One important implication from the body of research that employs cultural capital and habitus is that teachers', faculty members', and administrators' expectations play a huge role in determining students' eventual educational aspirations and life chances. The implication is that beginning to encourage students to reach higher aspirations, for example, may actually lead them to reach higher goals. It also implies a great deal of responsibility on the part of educational practitioners to be aware of their own biases and prejudices when it comes to which students they feel are "high ability," "meritorious, " or "smart."

Another result of educational research on this topic is that an educational institution (field) can have its own habitus (see, for example, McDonough's, 1997, work on college choice processes for students in various high schools). An educational setting (those in it) can impart aspirations to attend college to students, for example. Or on the contrary, an educational setting and those in it can discourage students from excelling, discouraging students' aspirations and educational possibilities. Thus, the importance of assessing an institutional habitus cannot be stressed too much. One way to consider the institutional habitus is to contemplate what students do after they leave the educational setting: Do they go on to college? Do they go to graduate school? Part of this assessment is also exploring the way that "merit" and "achievement" are identified in the institution.

Social Capital and Educational Practitioners

Although an analysis of social capital research was not the main goal of this monograph, some implications can still be garnered from the studies reviewed. The research suggests that students who come from backgrounds with social networks connected to colleges, universities, and schools will do better. This implies the importance of reconsidering legacy admissions in higher education or private secondary schools, for example. How do these types of admissions decisions privilege those who have social capital that is valued in educational contexts? This issue gets complicated quickly: in the example of legacy admissions, funding (private donations) is often associated with these social networks (for example, if a student is admitted whose family previously attended the institution, the likelihood is greater that the family will donate money to the institution). Even so, exploring the production and reproduction of social capital in an educational setting is necessary to take the research findings seriously in terms of applying them to educational practice.

Perhaps one of the most important implications related to the study of Bourdieu's notion of social capital in educational contexts is that educational practitioners can become a source of social capital for students. Hence, faculty, teachers, and administrators have a duty to connect students to other successful students and to those who might be able to afford students the social networks that they need. It is also necessary to better connect educational institutions to communities in considering the implications of social capital research. In other words, for educational practitioners to have the capability to connect students to particular social networks, they themselves must somehow be connected outside of their institution or at least know of others with whom students could connect.

The Continued Importance of Financial Capital

Along with the practical application of Bourdieu's concepts and the treatment of them in educational research, it is important for educational practitioners not to forget the continued importance of financial capital. In the end, Bourdieu's theoretical framework is rooted in the notion that the real disparities in material wealth eventually result in differences in cultural capital that are rewarded and appropriated in education.

It is therefore crucial for educational practitioners to inquire into the actual financial resources that may affect students' abilities to succeed in education and then to reflect on the ways that these resources (or lack thereof) influence cultural capital, habitus, and social capital. Educational practitioners should not take for granted that all students have the resources to purchase appropriate educational materials—or even for their basic survival needs like food and clothing. In primary and secondary schools, teachers and administrators should be aware of students who might not be eating at lunchtime, for example. Are some students not eating at lunchtime because they choose not to or because they do not have food available? Although free and reduced-price school lunch programs are available, many students (and their parents) may not want to apply because they sense some stigma is associated with it or because they do not know about the program. Teachers need to be alert to other basic survival needs for K–12 students: coats in the winter, food on the weekends, appropriate clothing or resources for activities (tennis shoes, band instruments, participation and lab fees). Has the teacher or administrator communicated with students privately about the availability of resources? Does the student own the necessary equipment to complete assignments—a computer, appropriate computer software, the required books and paper?

In postsecondary institutions, do students possess the resources or financial aid required for tuition, room, and board? If not, how is the student compensating for this lack of resources? Does the student possess the resources to be involved in the institution (participation fees, money for clothing, and so on)? Many students' success in higher education is directly linked to their financial resources, and they may have to compensate for the lack of financial resources by working part time or full time (also see St. John, 2006).

After considering a student's financial background and the way it might influence educational opportunities, institutional leaders need to take action on the findings. It may not mean needing more money so much as putting the financial resources toward the right support services for students (also see Winkle-Wagner, 2008). For example, in higher education, need-based financial aid programs that also come with stipends for living expenses might be necessary for many students. In K–12 schools, some communities have started sending food home in backpacks with low-income children over the weekends so that they do not go hungry for two days each week.[5]

Conclusion

Cultural capital has in many ways transformed the way that educational inequalities have been studied. Although interpreting and applying Bourdieu's ideas certainly have limitations, at the end of the day, I would argue more for extending, advancing, and reconsidering the concepts than ceasing to use them altogether.

All told, the potential pitfalls of cultural capital can potentially be mitigated by clearly defining what is meant by "cultural capital" both theoretically and in empirical applications of it; reassessing the limitations (and potential) of using an economic metaphor in the research process itself; unambiguously highlighting what cultural capital (and the related Bourdieuian framework) do and do not help to explain in educational settings; using Bourdieu's full theoretical structure, including the concepts of field and habitus in particular; thinking carefully about moral boundaries, race, and gender categories relative to Bourdieu's theoretical edifice, even if it requires new theorizing; remaining aware of the potential for a deficiency approach and attempting to avoid this snare; and reconsidering cultural capital in pluralistic contexts like the United States.

In terms of identifying the way that some groups continue to be privileged over others in seemingly tacit ways, cultural capital is an excellent theoretical framework and analytical tool. Related to education, cultural capital does provide a compelling explanation for the way that cultural status signals (often high-status signals) are rewarded in schools or postsecondary settings, giving students primarily from high socioeconomic status backgrounds an often imperceptible but very real edge over their peers. The idea of cultural capital does shift thinking in education toward structural notions of acquisition and perpetuation of privilege and inequality. Cultural capital can be helpful in identifying the "currency" that some students have and other students do not possess in educational settings.

Maybe the promise in Bourdieu's work, and in conflict theories more generally, is in the class conflict itself. That is to say, through class conflict and struggle shines a glimmer of hope that eventually the unequal distribution of rewards may be revolutionized. Bourdieu concludes his landmark work, *Distinction: A Social Critique of the Judgment of Taste* (1979a/1984), perhaps a bit skeptically: "The individual or collective classification struggles aimed at transforming the categories of perception and appreciation of the social world, and through this, the social world itself, are indeed a forgotten dimension of the class struggle" (p. 484).

Although class struggle that has the potential to transform the social structure might be a "forgotten dimension," it does not necessarily mean that struggle (and revolution, for that matter) cannot be recalled. As Kingston (2001) put it, Bourdieu's theoretical posture implies that educational institutions "could be organized by other, more inclusive cultural principles" (p. 90). This reorganization might be one of the unmet promises of cultural capital and class struggle more generally—the identification of a way that new forms of cultural capital might be better recognized and rewarded in education. This promise and the hope inspired by it suggest an important charge for future empirical, theoretical, and practical work in educational settings.

Notes

1. This agency-structure interaction in Bourdieu's theorizing differentiated him from arguments like Oscar Lewis's "Culture of Poverty" (1998), for example.
2. This argument assumes that educational attainment directly correlates to occupational status. In the United States, noteworthy exceptions exist (for example, Bill Gates, who does not have a college degree).
3. Turner (1960) compared the British and American educational systems, likening them to "sponsorship" (in the case of the British system) or a "contest" (in the case of the American educational system). The contest is rooted in meritocratic thinking in which position and outcomes should be based on merit, the rules are clear, the "contest" is accessible to all, the contest is rooted in competition, and multiple elites exist so many people can attempt to compete for elite status. Sponsorship, on the other hand, implies that one must be "sponsored" to gain entry into the educational system, the rules are not transparent, the system is not accessible to the masses, and only one elite status exists, so many people cannot attempt to gain this status (unless they are sponsored to do so).
4. Although Bowles and Gintis argued later (2002) that they were not functionalist in their orientation, their work has generally been interpreted that way.
5. For more information on the BackPack Program, see http://feeding america.org/our-network/network-programs/backpack-program.aspx

References

Anderson, G. M. (2005). In the name of diversity: Education and the commoditization and consumption of race in the United States. *Urban Review, 5*(37), 399–423.

Aries, E., and Seider, M. (2005). The interactive relationship between class identity and the college experience: The case of lower income students. *Qualitative Sociology, 28*(4), 419–433.

Arnold, K. D. (2002). Getting to the top: What role do elite colleges play? *About Campus, 7*(5), 4–12.

Aschaffenburg, K., and Maas, I. (1997). Cultural and educational careers: The dynamics of social reproduction. *American Sociological Review, 62*(4), 573–587.

Astin, A. W., and Oseguera, L. (2004). The declining "equity" of American higher education. *Review of Higher Education, 27*(3), 321–341.

Banton, M. (1998). *Racial theories* (2nd ed.). New York: Cambridge University Press.

Becker, G. S. (1993). *Human capital: A theoretical and empirical analysis with special reference to education* (3rd ed.). Chicago: University of Chicago Press.

Bills, D. B. (2003). Credentials, signals, and screens: Explaining the relationship between schooling and job assignment. *Review of Educational Research, 4*(73), 441–469.

Blau, J. (2004). *Race in the School: Perpetuating white dominance?* Boulder, CO: Lynne Rienner Publishers.

Bourdieu, P. (1971/1977). Cultural reproduction and social reproduction. In J. Karabel and A. H. Halsey (Eds.), *Power and ideology in education* (pp. 487–511). New York: Oxford University Press.

Bourdieu, P. (1973). Cultural reproduction and social reproduction. In R. Brown (Ed.), *Knowledge, education and cultural change: Papers in the sociology of education* (pp. 71–112). London: Taylor & Francis.

Bourdieu, P. (1977). *Outline of a theory of practice.* R. Nice (Trans.). Cambridge, UK: Cambridge University Press.

Bourdieu, P. (1979a/1984). *Distinction: A social critique of the judgment of taste.* R. Nice (Trans.). Cambridge, MA: Harvard University Press.

Bourdieu, P. (1979b/1987). The forms of capital. In J. G. Richardson (Ed.), *Handbook of theory and research for the sociology of education*. New York: Greenwood.

Bourdieu, P. (1990). *The logic of practice*. Stanford, CA: Stanford University Press.

Bourdieu, P. (1993). *Sociology in question*. Thousand Oaks, CA: Sage.

Bourdieu, P. (1994). *Language and symbolic power*. Cambridge, MA: Harvard University Press.

Bourdieu, P., and Passeron, J.-C. (1964/1979). *The inheritors: French students and their relation to culture*. Chicago: University of Chicago Press.

Bourdieu, P., and Passeron, J.-C. (1970/1977, reprinted 1990). *Reproduction in education, society and culture*. Beverly Hills, CA: Sage.

Bourdieu, P., and Wacquant, L.J.D. (1992). *An invitation to reflexive sociology*. Chicago: University of Chicago Press.

Bowles, S., and Gintis, H. (1976). Beyond the educational frontier: The great American dream machine. *Schooling in Capitalist America: Educational reform and the contradictions of economic life*. New York: Basic.

Bowles, S., and Gintis, H. (2002). Schooling in capitalist America revisited. *Sociology of Education, 75*, 1–18.

Brändström, S. (1999). Music education as investment in cultural capital. *Research Studies in Music Education, 12*(1), 49–57.

Brooks, R., and Everett, G. (2008). New European learners? An analysis of the "trendsetter" thesis. *Journal of Youth Studies, 11*(4), 377–391.

Bullen, E., and Kenway, J. (2005). Bourdieu, subcultural capital and risky girlhood. *Theory and Research in Education, 3*(1), 47–61.

Cabrera, A. F., and La Nasa, S. M. (2001). On the path to college: Three critical tasks facing America's disadvantaged. *Research in Higher Education, 42*(2), 119–149.

Carspecken, P. F. (1996). *Critical ethnography in educational research: A theoretical and practical guide*. New York: Routledge.

Carter, P. L. (2003). "Black" cultural capital, status positioning and schooling conflicts for low-income African American youth. *Social Problems, 50*(1), 136–155.

Charmaz, K. (2005). Grounded theory in the 21st century: Applications for advancing social justice studies. In N. K. Denzin and Y. S. Lincoln (Eds.), *The SAGE handbook of qualitative research* (3rd ed., pp. 507–536). London: Sage Publications.

Cheadle, J. E. (2008). Educational investment, family contest, and children's math and reading growth from kindergarten through the third grade. *Sociology of Education, 81*(1), 1–31.

Christ, T., and Wang, X. C. (2008). Negotiation of "how to" at the cross-section of cultural capital and habitus: Young children's procedural practices in a student-led literacy group. *Journal of Early Childhood Literacy, 8*(2), 177–211.

Coleman, J. (1988). Social capital in the creation of human capital. *American Journal of Sociology, 94*, 95–121.

Collier, P. J., and Morgan, D. L. (2008). "Is that paper really due today?" Differences in first-generation and traditional college students' understandings of faculty expectations. *Higher Education, 55*, 425–446.

Collins, R. (1971). Functional and conflict theories of educational stratification. *American Sociological Review, 36,* 1002–1019.

Conley, D. (1999/2010). *Being Black, living in the red.* Berkeley: University of California Press.

Cookson, P. W., and Persell, C. (1985). *Preparing for power: America's elite boarding schools.* New York: Basic.

Creswell, J. W. (1998). *Qualitative inquiry and research design: Choosing among the five traditions.* Thousand Oaks: Sage.

Dar, Y., and Getz, S. (2007). Learning ability, socioeconomic status and student placement for undergraduate studies in Israel. *Higher Education, 54*(1), 41–60.

Davies, S., and Guppy, N. (1997). Fields of study, college selectivity, and student inequalities in higher education. *Social Forces, 75*(4), 1413–1438.

Davis, K., and Moore, W. (1945). Some principles of stratification. *American Sociological Review, 10,* 242–249.

Deem, R. (2006). Changing research perspectives on the management of higher education: Can research permeate the activities of manager-academics? *Higher Education Quarterly, 3*(60), 203–228.

De Graaf, N. D., De Graaf, P. M., and Kraaykamp, G. (2000). Parental cultural capital and educational attainment in the Netherlands: A refinement of the cultural capital perspective. *Sociology of Education, 73*(2), 92–111.

De Graaf, P. M. (1986). The impact of financial and cultural resources on educational attainment in the Netherlands. *Sociology of Education, 59,* 237–246.

Denzin, N. K., and Lincoln, Y. S. (Eds.). (2003). *The landscape of qualitative research: Theories and issues* (2nd ed.). Thousand Oaks: Sage.

Devas, A. (2004). Reflection as confession: Discipline and docility in/on the student body. *Art Design and Communication in Higher Education, 3*(1), 33–46.

De Vries, J., and De Graaf, P. M. (2008). Is the intergenerational transmission of higher cultural activities biased by the retrospective measurement of parental high cultural activities? *Social Indicators Research, 85,* 311–327.

DiMaggio, P. (1982). Cultural capital and school success: The impact of status culture participation on the grades of U.S. high school students. *American Sociological Review, 47*(2), 189–201.

DiMaggio, P., and Mohr, J. (1985). Cultural capital, educational attainment and marital selection. *American Journal of Sociology, 90*(6), 1231–1985.

Driessen, G.W.J.M. (2001). Ethnicity, forms of capital, and educational achievement. *International Review of Education, 47*(6), 513–538.

Dumais, S. A. (2002). Cultural capital, gender and school success: The role of habitus. *Sociology of Education, 75*(1), 44–68.

Dumais, S. A. (2006). Early childhood cultural capital, parental habitus and teachers' perceptions. *Poetics: Journal of Empirical Research on Literature, the Media and Arts, 34*(2), 83–107.

Eitle, T. M., and Eitle, D. J. (2002). Race, cultural capital and the educational effects of participation in sports. *Sociology of Education, 75*(2), 123–143.

English, F. W. (2002). On the intractability of the achievement gap in urban schools and the discursive practice of continuing racial discrimination. *Education and Urban Society, 34*(3), 298–311.

Evans, S. (2009). In a different place: Working-class girls and higher education. *Sociology, 43*(2), 340–355.

Farkas, G. (2003). Cognitive skills and noncognitive traits and behaviors in stratification processes. *Annual Review of Sociology, 29*(1), 541–562.

Farkas, G., Grobe, R. P., Sheehan, D., and Shuan, Y. (1990). Cultural resources and school success: Gender, ethnicity and poverty groups within an urban school district. *American Sociological Review, 55*(1), 127–142.

Franklin, V. P. (2002). Cultural capital and African American education. *Journal of African American History, 87*(2), 175–181.

Freeman, K. (1997). Increasing African Americans' participation in higher education: African American high-school students' perspectives. *Journal of Higher Education, 68*(5), 523–551.

García, S. B., and Guerra, P. L. (2004). Deconstructing deficit thinking: Working with educators to create more equitable learning environments. *Education and Urban Society, 36*(2), 150–168.

Gilbourn, D. (2005). Education policy as an act of White supremacy: Whiteness, critical race theory and education reform. *Journal of Education Policy, 4,* 485–505.

Glaser, B. G., and Strauss, A. L. (1967). *The discovery of grounded theory: Strategies for qualitative research.* London: Weidenfeld & Nicolson.

Goldstein, T. (2003). *Teaching and learning in a multilingual school: Choices, risks, and dilemmas.* Mahwah, NJ: Erlbaum.

Goyette, K. A., and Mullen, A. L. (2006). Who studies the arts and sciences? Social background and consequences of undergraduate field of study. *Journal of Higher Education, 77*(3), 497–539.

Gregory, E., Williams, A., Baker, D., and Street, B. (2004). Introducing literacy to four year olds: Creating classroom cultures in three schools. *Journal of Early Childhood Literacy, 4*(1), 85–107.

Gvion, L., and Luzzatto, D. (2008). Affluent parent's advocacy for special-education children's rights vis-à-vis placement committees in Israel. *Education, Citizenship and Social Justice, 2*(3), 147–166.

Harper, S. R., and Hurtado, S. (2007). Nine themes in campus racial climates and implications for institutional transformation. In S. R. Harper and L. D. Patton (Eds.), *Responding to the realities of race on campus.* New Directions for Student Services (No. 120, pp. 7–24). San Francisco: Jossey-Bass.

Holt, D. B. (1998). Does cultural capital structure American consumption? *Journal of Consumer Research, 1*(25), 1–25.

Horvat, E. M. (1997, March). "Structure, standpoint and practices: The construction and meaning of the boundaries of blackness for African American female high school seniors in the college choice process." Paper presented at an annual meeting of the American Educational Research Association, Chicago. (ED 407 884)

Horvat, E. M. (2001). Understanding equity and access in higher education: The potential contribution of Pierre Bourdieu. In J. C. Smart (Ed.), *Higher education: Handbook of theory and practice*. New York: Agathon.

Horvat, E. M. (2003). The interactive effects of race and class in educational research: Theoretical insights from the work of Pierre Bourdieu. *Penn GSE Perspectives on Urban Education, 2*(1), 1–25.

Kalmijn, M., and Kraaykamp, G. (1996). Race, cultural capital and schooling: An analysis of trends in the United States. *Sociology of Education, 69*(1), 22–34.

Karen, D. (1991). "Achievement" and "ascription" in admission to an elite college: A political-organizational analysis. *Sociological Forum, 6*(2), 349–380.

Katsillis, J., and Rubinson, R. (1990). Cultural capital, student achievement and educational reproduction: The case of Greece. *American Sociological Review, 55*(2), 270–279.

Kaufman, J., and Gabler, J. (2004). Cultural capital and the extracurricular activities of girls and boys in the college attainment process. *Poetics: Journal of Empirical Research on Literature, the Media and Arts, 32*(2), 145–168.

Kingston, P. W. (2000). *The classless society*. Stanford, CA: Stanford University Press.

Kingston, P. W. (2001). The unfulfilled promise of cultural capital theory. *Sociology of Education, 74*, 88–99.

Lamont, M. (1992). *Money, morals, and manners: The culture of the French and the American upper-middle class*. Chicago: University of Chicago Press.

Lamont, M., Kaufman, J., and Moody, M. (2000). The best of the brightest: Definitions of the ideal self among prize-winning students. *Sociological Forum, 15*(2), 187–224.

Lamont, M., and Lareau, A. (1988). Cultural capital: Allusions, gaps and glissandos in recent theoretical developments. *Sociological Theory, 6*(2), 153–168.

Lareau, A. (1987). Social class differences in family-school relationships: The importance of cultural capital. *Sociology of Education, 60*(2), 73–85.

Lareau, A. (2000). *Home advantage: Social class and parental intervention in elementary education*. Philadelphia: Palmer Press.

Lareau, A. (2003). *Unequal childhoods: Class, race, and family life*. Los Angeles: University of California Press.

Lareau, A., and Horvat, E. M. (1999). Moments of social inclusion and exclusion: Race, class and cultural capital in family-school relationships. *Sociology of Education, 72*(1), 37–53.

Lareau, A., and Weininger, E. B. (2003). Cultural capital in educational research: A critical assessment. *Theory and Society, 32*, 567–606.

Lee, J., and Bowen, N. K. (2006). Parent involvement, cultural capital and the achievement gap among elementary school children. *American Educational Research Journal, 43*(2), 193–218.

Lee, V. E., and Burkam, D. T. (2002). *Inequality at the starting gate: Social background differences in achievement as children begin school*. Washington, D.C.: Economic Policy Institute.

Leibowitz, B. (2009). What's inside the suitcases? An investigation into the powerful resources students and lecturers bring to teaching and learning. *Higher Education Research and Development, 28*(3), 261–274.

Lewis, O. (1998). Culture of poverty. *Society, 35*(2), 7–9.

Lundberg, C. A. (2007). A bleacher-seat view of cultural capital: How bad is a dented bat? *About Campus, 11*(6), 8–2.

Martin, N. D., and Spenner, K. I. (2009). Capital conversion and accumulation: A social portrait of legacies at an elite university. *Research in Higher Education, 50*(7), 623–648.

Martinez-Cosio, M., and Iannacone, R. M. (2007). The tenuous role of institutional agents: Parent liaisons as cultural brokers. *Education and Urban Society, 39*(3), 349–369.

McDonough, P. M. (1994). Buying and selling higher education: The social construction of the college applicant. *The Journal of Higher Education, 65*(4), 427–446.

McDonough, P. M. (1997). *Choosing colleges: How social class and schools structure opportunity.* Albany: State University of New York Press.

McDonough, P. M., Korn, J., and Yamasaki, E. (1997). Access, equity and the privatization of college counseling. *Review of Higher Education, 20*(3), 297–317.

McDonough, P. M., Ventresca, M., and Outcalt, C. (1999). Fields of dreams: Understanding sociohistorical changes in college access, 1965–1995. In J. C. Smart (Ed.), *Higher education: Handbook of theory and research* (vol. 15). New York: Agathon.

McNeal, R. B. (1999). Parental involvement as social capital: Differential effectiveness on science, achievement, truancy, and dropping out. *Social Forces, 78,* 117–144.

Meerabeau, E. (2006). Poor relations? Nursing and medicine in the English academy. *Higher Education Quarterly, 60*(1), 52–73.

Modood, T. (2004). Capitals, ethnic identity and educational qualifications. *Cultural Trends, 13*(2), 87–105.

Mohr, J., and Dimaggio, P. (1995). The intergenerational transmission of cultural capital. *Research in Social Stratification and Mobility, 14,* 167–199.

Monkman, K., Ronald, M., and Délimon Théramène, F. (2005). Social and cultural capital in an urban Latino school community. *Urban Education, 40*(1), 4–33.

Moore, R. (2004). Cultural capital: Objective probability and the cultural arbitrary. *British Journal of Sociology of Education, 25*(4), 445–456.

Musoba, G., and Baez, B. (2009). The cultural capital of cultural and social capital: An economy of translations. In J. C. Smart (Ed.), *Higher education: Handbook of theory and research* (vol. 24). New York: Agathon.

Nasir, N. S., and Saxe, G. B. (2003). Ethnic and academic identities: A cultural practice perspective on emerging tensions and their management in the lives of minority students. *Educational Researcher, 5*(32), 14–18.

Noble, J., and Davies, P. (2009). Cultural capital as an explanation of variation in participation in higher education. *British Journal of Sociology of Education, 30*(5), 591–605.

Nora, A. (2004). The role of habitus and cultural capital in choosing a college, transitioning from high school to higher education, and persisting in college among minority and non-minority students. *Journal of Hispanic Higher Education, 2*(3), 180–208.

Núñez, A. M. (2009). Modeling the effects of diversity experiences and multiple capitals on Latina/o college students' academic self-confidence. *Journal of Hispanic Higher Education, 8*(2), 179–196.

Oakes, J. (1985). *Keeping track*. New Haven, CT: Yale University Press.

Oakes, J., Wells, A. S., Jones, M., and Datnow, A. (1997). Detracking: The social construction of ability, cultural politics and resistance to reform. *Teachers College Record, 98*(2), 482–510.

Olneck, M. (2000). Can multicultural education change what counts as cultural capital? *American Educational Research Journal, 2*(37), 317–348.

O'Shea, A. (1998). A special relationship? Cultural studies, academia and pedagogy. *Cultural Studies, 4*(12), 513–527.

Oliver, M. L., and Shapiro, T. M. (1997). *Black wealth/White wealth: A new perspective on racial inequality*. New York: Routledge.

Pascarella, E. T., Pierson, C. T., Wolniak, G. C, and Terenzini, P. T. (2004). First-generation college students: Additional evidence on college experiences and outcomes. *Journal of Higher Education, 75*(3), 249–284.

Patiniotis, J., and Holdsworth, C. (2005). "Seize that chance!" Leaving home and transitions to higher education. *Journal of Youth Studies, 1*(8), 81–95.

Pearce, R. R., and Lin, Z. (2005). Cultural capital and postsecondary educational attainment among White and Chinese Americans: An analysis of NELS 1988–2000. *Educational Review, 1*(59), 19–36.

Pearce, R. R., and Lin, Z. (2007). Chinese-American postsecondary achievement and attainment: A cultural and structural analysis. *Educational Review, 59*(1), 19–36.

Perna, L. W. (2000). Differences in the decision to attend college among African Americans, Hispanics, and Whites. *Journal of Higher Education, 71*(2), 117–141.

Perna, L. W., and Titus, M. A. (2005). The relationship between parental involvement as social capital and college enrollment: An examination of racial/ethnic group differences. *Journal of Higher Education, 76*(5), 486–518.

Peterson, R., and Kern, R. M. (1996). Changing highbrow taste: From snob to omnivore. *American Sociological Review, 61*(5), 900–907.

Pradl, G. M. (2002). Linking instructional intervention and professional development: Using the ideas behind Puente High School English to inform educational policy. *Educational Policy, 16*(4), 522–546.

Robbins, D. (1991). *The work of Pierre Bourdieu*. Boulder, CO: Westview Press.

Robinson, R. V., and Garnier, M. A. (1985). Class reproduction among men and women in France: Reproduction theory on its home ground. *American Journal of Sociology, 91*(2), 250–280.

Roscigno, V. J., and Ainsworth-Darnell, J. W. (1999). Race, cultural capital and educational resources: Persistent inequalities and achievement returns. *Sociology of Education, 72*(3), 158–178.

Russell, J. (2006). Inuit student teachers' agency, positioning and symbolic action: Reflections from a Qallunaat on music teaching in the Canadian Arctic. *International Journal of Music Education, 3*(24), 231–242.

St. John, E. P. (2006). *Education and the public interest: School reform, public finance, and access to higher education*. Dordrecht, the Netherlands: Springer.

Salisbury, M. H., Umbach, P. D., Paulsen, M. B., and Pascarella, E. T. (2009). Going global: Understanding the choice process of the intent to study abroad. *Research in Higher Education, 50*(2), 119–143.

Saunders, M., and Serna, I. (2004). Making college happen: The college experiences of first-generation Latino students. *Journal of Hispanic Higher Education, 3*(2), 146–163.

Schultz, T. W. (1961). Investment in human capital. *American Economic Review, 51*(1), 1–17.

Shapiro, T. M. (2004). *The hidden cost of being African American: How wealth perpetuates inequality.* New York: Oxford University Press.

Smrekar, C. (1996). *The impact of school choice and community: In the interest of families and schools.* Albany: State University of New York Press.

Span, C. M. (2002). I must learn now or not at all: Social and cultural capital in the educational initiatives of formerly enslaved African Americans in Mississippi, 1862–1869. *Journal of African American History, 87*, 196–205.

Stanton-Salazar, R. D., and Dornbusch, S. M. (1995). Social capital and the reproduction of inequality: Information networks among Mexican-origin high school students. *Sociology of Education, 68*(2), 113–135.

Steelman, L. C., and Powell, B. (1989). Acquiring capital for college: The constraints of family configuration. *American Sociological Review, 54*(5), 844–855.

Strange, C. C., and Banning, J. H. (2001). *Educating by design: Creating campus learning environments that work.* San Francisco: Jossey-Bass.

Sullivan, A. (2001). Cultural capital and educational attainment. *Sociology, 35*(4), 893–912.

Swartz, D. (1997). *Culture and power: The sociology of Pierre Bourdieu.* Chicago: University of Chicago Press.

Tierney, W. G. (1999). Models of minority college-going and retention: Cultural integrity versus cultural suicide. *Journal of Negro Education, 68*, 80–91.

Tierney, W. G. (2002). Parents and families in precollege preparation: The lack of connection between research and practice. *Educational Policy, 4*(16), 588–606.

Tomusk, V. (2000). Reproduction of the "state nobility" in Eastern Europe: Past patterns and new practices. *British Journal of Sociology of Education, 21*(2), 269–282.

Topper, K. (2001). Not so trifling nuances: Pierre Bourdieu, symbolic violence and the perversions of democracy. *Constellations, 8*, 30–56.

Torres, V., Howard-Hamilton, M. F., and Cooper, D. L. (Eds.) (2003). Identity development of diverse populations: Implications for teaching and administration in higher education. *ASHE-ERIC Higher Education Report, 29*(6).

Turner, R. H. (1960). Sponsored and contest mobility and the school system. *American Sociological Review, 25*(6), 855–867.

Valadez, J. (1993). Cultural capital and its impact on the aspirations of nontraditional community college students. *Community College Review, 21*(3), 30–43.

Valenzuela, A. (1999). *Subtractive schooling: U.S.-Mexican youth and the politics of caring.* New York: SUNY Press.

Walpole, M. (2003). Socioeconomic status and college: How SES affects college experiences and outcomes. *Review of Higher Education, 1*(27), 45–73.

Walpole, M., McDonough, P. M., Bauer, C. J., Gibson, C., Kanyi, K., and Toliver, R. (2005). This test is unfair: Urban African American and Latino high school students' perceptions of standardized admission tests. *Urban Education, 40*(3), 321–349.

Walton, M., and Archer, A. (2004). The web and information literacy: Scaffolding the use of web sources in a project-based curriculum. *British Journal of Educational Technology, 35*(2), 176–186.

Weininger, E. B., and Lareau, A. (2003). Translating Bourdieu into the American context: The question of social class and family-school relations. *Poetics: Journal of Empirical Research on Literature, the Media and Arts, 31*, 375–402.

Wells, R. (2008). The effects of social and cultural capital on student persistence: Are community colleges more meritocratic? *Community College Review, 36*(1), 25–46.

Winkle-Wagner, R. (2008). Putting money in the right places: Policy suggestions for supporting first-generation African American women in college. *ASHE–Lumina Policy Brief Series*, 6.

Winkle-Wagner, R. (2009a). The perpetual homelessness of college experiences: The tensions between home and campus for African American women. *Review of Higher Education, 33*(1), 1–36.

Winkle-Wagner, R. (2009b). *The unchosen me: Race, gender, and identity among Black women in college.* Baltimore: Johns Hopkins University Press.

Yosso, T. J. (2005). Whose culture has capital? A critical race theory discussion of community cultural wealth. *Race Ethnicity and Education, 8*(1), 69–91.

Zarycki, T. (2007). Cultural capital and the accessibility of higher education. *Russian Education and Society, 49*(7), 41–72.

Zarycki, T. (2009). Cultural capital and the political orientations of the younger generation of the Russian and Polish intelligentsia. *Russian Education and Society, 51*(2), 3–43.

Zweigenhaft, R. L. (1993). Prep school and public school graduates of Harvard: A longitudinal study of the accumulation of social and cultural capital. *Journal of Higher Education 64*(2), 211–225.

Name Index

A

Ainsworth-Darnell, J. W., 1, 2, 30, 34, 35, 36, 37, 66, 68, 79, 81
Anderson, G. M., 31, 39, 44
Archer, A., 31
Aries, E., 31, 39, 40, 42, 45, 67
Arnold, K. D., 31, 44
Aschaffenburg, K., 30, 35, 36, 37, 66
Astin, A. W., 31, 39, 40, 43

B

Baez, B., 3, 4, 19, 32, 49, 60, 61, 74, 77, 81, 82
Baker, D., 31, 39, 40
Banning, J. H., 105
Banton, M., 73
Bauer, C. J., 32, 49, 67
Becker, G. S., 60
Bills, D. B., 31
Blau, J., 77
Bourdieu, P., 3, 4–6, 7, 8, 9, 11, 12, 13, 14, 15, 16, 17, 18, 19, 20, 62, 64, 69, 74, 78, 82, 89, 91, 92, 98, 100, 111
Bowen, N. K., 32, 49
Bowles, S., 63, 113
Brändström, S., 30
Brooks, R., 32
Bullen, E., 32, 97
Burkam, D. T., 77

C

Cabrera, A. F., 2, 31, 34

Carspecken, P. F., 88, 95
Carter, P. L., 32, 39, 45, 46, 48
Charmaz, K., 64, 88
Cheadle, J. E., 2, 31, 34, 40, 41, 45, 67, 76, 81, 87, 102
Christ, T., 32
Coleman, J., 42, 86–87
Collier, P. J., 30, 38, 67, 68, 70, 84
Collins, R., 61, 62
Conley, D., 65, 100
Cookson, P. W., 11, 54, 76, 81
Cooper, D. L., 72
Creswell, J. W., 88

D

Dar, Y., 30
Datnow, A., 31, 39, 40, 41
Davies, P., 30, 86, 102, 103
Davies, S., 2, 31, 34
Davis, K., 61
De Graaf, N. D., 30, 35
De Graaf, P. M., 30, 35
De Vries, J., 30
Deem, R., 32
Délimon Théramène, F., 32, 49
Denzin, N. K., 88
Devas, A., 30
DiMaggio, P., 1, 2, 14, 30, 33, 34, 35, 36, 39, 66, 75, 81
Dornbusch, S. M., 31
Driessen, G.W.J.M., 30
Dumais, S. A., 2, 31, 32, 80

Subject Index

A

Abuses of cultural capital, 23–57

Academic Search Premier, 24

Acquisition of cultural capital, 6

African American students: achievement gap between White students and, 37; college choice process, 42; cultural capital, importance to, 50; disadvantage relative to cultural capital acquisition, 68; educational rewards, 68; knowledge of college admissions exams as marker for cultural capital/habitus, 56; social capital, 51

Agency-structural gap, 63

Agency-structure interaction, 4–5, 16–17, 113

American country context, of cultural capital, 100–101

Analysis, methodological, 23–27

B

BackPack program, 110, 113

"Black" cultural capital of African American youth, 46

"Bootstrap" mentality, 83

Bourdieu, P., 3, 4–9, 11–21, 23–29, 33–35, 38, 40, 44, 46, 48–53, 55–57, 59–65, 74–83, 85, 86, 88–90, 92–99, 101, 102, 104–105, 107, 108–111, 113; *Distinction: A Social Critique of the Judgment of Taste*, 64–65, 74; *doxa*, 17; economic metaphor, 69–72; linking theory and data, and the macro- and microlevels, 63–65; *Reproduction in Education, Society and Culture*, 20; social capital, 12–13; social conditioning formula, 15–17; social distinction, 13–15; sociology, 3–5, theory of the reproduction of inequality, 5; theory of social reproduction, 93–96

Bourdieuian framework cultural capital, 29, 33, 48–57, 59; college choice processes, 55–56; college student retention, 56–57; cultural capital and social capital, 49–53; cultural capital, field, and habitus, 53–57; influences of high school counselors/families on college choice process, 55

C

Chinese Americans, cultural capital of, 47–48

Class, 2–3

Class-based privilege and a pluralistic society, 73–78

Classifying practices, 11–12

Community cultural wealth, 71

Conflict theory, 3, 61–62

Contest, 83, 113

Contest system of education, 19

Contextually-valued cultural capital, 29, 33, 39–45; aspirations of nontraditional students (Valadez), 42; college choice process of African American high school students (Freeman), 42; college experiences of Latino students (Saunders/Serna), 44; detracking efforts in schools (Oakes/Wells/Jones/Datnow), 41; educational issues examined using, 40–41; examination of informal academic standards (Farkas), 40–41; examining cultural capital relative to the accumulation of privilege (Anderson), 44; family income role in considerations of cultural capital (St. John), 43; hierarchical modeling with Early Childhood Longitudinal Study data (Cheadle), 41–42; identity of lower-income students at elite and state college (Aries/Seider), 42–43; inequalities between types of institutions and programs (Astin/Oseguera), 43; multilevel statistical modeling, 45; nuance of interpretation, 44

Country context, of cultural capital, 99–101

Cultural capital: absence of full theory in empirical work, 88–89; acquisition of, 6; applications/interpretations of, 59–90; Bourdieuian framework, 29, 33; Bourdieu's intent with, 70–71; Bourdieu's theory of, 78; card-game metaphor, 6; communal definition of, 46; contextually-valued, 29, 33; country context of, 99–101; cultural wealth, 14; defined, viii, 5–7, 27–34, 92–93; economic metaphor of, 69–72; and education, 17–21; and educational attainment, 19; in educational research, 34–57; embodied, 76; empirical test of, 24; field, 7–8; as form of goods in educational settings, vii; future of, 91–111; and gender, 96–99; habitus, 8–11; at heart of scholarly analysis, 101–102; highbrow, 29, 33; as it relates to education, 24; lessons from, in extant educational research, 65–68; literature, by definition/education milieu, 30–33; measurement of, 84; merits of, in educational research, 59–68; methodological limitations of, 85–89; and

moral boundaries, 72–73; objectified, 75–76; origins of idea, 2–3; otherized, 29, 33; promises/pitfalls in educational research, 21; and race, 96–99; and reinforcement of meritocratic sensibilities, 83–84; social capital, 12–13; and social conditioning formula, 15–16; as a social relationship, 8; and social reproduction, 1–21; and social settings, 13; and structural forces, 62; studies, world map of, 28; substantive limitations of, 69–85; theoretical treatment of, 24; theory of social reproduction, 3–17; treatments of, 1–2; use of term, 2; uses/abuses of, 23–57

Cultural capital research, 101–104; definition and operationalization of, 86–88; educational practice applications of, 104–110; methodological considerations, 101–104; theoretical advancement relative to, 92–101

Cultural competence, use of term, 14

Cultural wealth, 14, 19; community, 71

Culturally based resources, vi

D

Distinction, 14

Distinction: A Social Critique of the Judgment of Taste (Bourdieu), 64–65, 74, 78, 82, 111

Diverse Democracy Project, 47

Domination: centrality of, 82–83; division of, 10; and racial equality, 100; theory of, 81–82

Domination theory, and deficiency applications, 81–86

Doxa, 17

E

Economic metaphor, 69–72; of cultural capital, 69–72

Education, and cultural capital, 17–21

Educational attainment: and cultural capital, 19; and occupational status, 113

Educational practice: applications, of cultural capital research, 104–110; cultural capital in, 105–106; field of,

American youth, 46; communal
definition of cultural capital, 46;
intercultural capital, 47; multicultural
education, and cultural capital, 47;
students of color, 46–47; theoretical
progression of cultural capital, 46–47

P

Parental cultural capital, 36–37
Parental involvement in education, and
college enrollment, 67
Pluralistic society, and homogeneous class-
based privilege, 73–78
Privilege, 4
Project Talent, 35

R

Race: absence of, 78–81; and cultural
capital, 96–99
Racial equality, and domination, 100
Racial groups, and morality, 73
Racial stratification, 78–81
Racism, 73

S

Social capital, 12–13; and educational
practitioners, 108
Social conditioning formula, 15–16
Social distinctions, 13–15; and symbolic
violence, 15
Social groups, and economic metaphor, 71–72
Social network, as credential in social
settings, 13
Social reproduction: and cultural capital,
1–21; theory of, 3–17
Social stratification, 4
Socioeconomic inequality, less tangible
aspects of, 60

Sponsored system of education, 19
Sponsorship, 83, 113
Student cultural capital, 36–37
Survey of Attitudes and Behaviors
Influencing College Choice, 56
Survey of Public Participation in the Arts, 36
Symbolic power, 13
Symbolic violence, 15

T

Taste, 11–12; and field, 12; as match-
maker, 12; zones of, 11
Theoretical advancement, relative to
cultural capital research, 92–101
Theoretical progression, of cultural capital,
46–47
Theoretical treatment, of cultural capital, 24
Theories: Bourdieu's theory of cultural
capital, 78; conflict, 3, 61–62; of
domination, 81–82; of the reproduction
of inequality, 5; of social reproduction,
3–17

U

*Unequal Childhoods: Class, Race, and Family
Life* (Lareau), 65
Uses of cultural capital in educational
research, 23–57

W

Wealth, cultural, 14, 19
Web of Science, 24
Work, division of, 10
World Map of Cultural Capital Studies, 28

Z

Zones of taste, 11

About the Author

Rachelle Winkle-Wagner is assistant professor of higher education in the Department of Educational Administration at the University of Nebraska in Lincoln. She received her Ph.D. from Indiana University in education policy studies with a concentration in higher education and minors in sociology and qualitative research methodology. Her research agenda centers on the sociological aspects of race and gender in higher education. She is the author of *The Unchosen Me: Race, Gender, and Identity Among Black Women in College* (2009, Johns Hopkins University Press), the lead editor of *Bridging the Gap Between Theory and Practice in Educational Research: Methods at the Margins* (2009, Palgrave MacMillan), and a coeditor of *Standing on the Outside Looking In: Underrepresented Students' Experiences in Advanced Degree Programs* (2009, Stylus Publishing). She has also published articles in *The Review of Higher Education, The International Journal of Educational Development, The Negro Educational Review,* and *Teachers College Record.*

About the ASHE Higher Education Report Series

Since 1983, the ASHE (formerly ASHE-ERIC) Higher Education Report Series has been providing researchers, scholars, and practitioners with timely and substantive information on the critical issues facing higher education. Each monograph presents a definitive analysis of a higher education problem or issue, based on a thorough synthesis of significant literature and institutional experiences. Topics range from planning to diversity and multiculturalism, to performance indicators, to curricular innovations. The mission of the Series is to link the best of higher education research and practice to inform decision making and policy. The reports connect conventional wisdom with research and are designed to help busy individuals keep up with the higher education literature. Authors are scholars and practitioners in the academic community. Each report includes an executive summary, review of the pertinent literature, descriptions of effective educational practices, and a summary of key issues to keep in mind to improve educational policies and practice.

The Series is one of the most peer reviewed in higher education. A National Advisory Board made up of ASHE members reviews proposals. A National Review Board of ASHE scholars and practitioners reviews completed manuscripts. Six monographs are published each year and they are approximately 120 pages in length. The reports are widely disseminated through Jossey-Bass and John Wiley & Sons, and they are available online to subscribing institutions through Wiley InterScience (http://www.interscience.wiley.com).

Call for Proposals

The ASHE Higher Education Report Series is actively looking for proposals. We encourage you to contact one of the editors, Dr. Kelly Ward (kaward@wsu.edu) or Dr. Lisa Wolf-Wendel (lwolf@ku.edu), with your ideas.

Recent Titles

ASHE HIGHER EDUCATION REPORT

ORDER FORM SUBSCRIPTION AND SINGLE ISSUES

DISCOUNTED BACK ISSUES:

Use this form to receive 20% off all back issues of *ASHE Higher Education Report*.
All single issues priced at **$23.20** (normally $29.00)

TITLE	ISSUE NO.	ISBN
_____	_____	_____
_____	_____	_____

Call 888-378-2537 or see mailing instructions below. When calling, mention the promotional code JBXND to receive your discount. For a complete list of issues, please visit www.josseybass.com/go/aehe

SUBSCRIPTIONS: (1 YEAR, 6 ISSUES)

☐ New Order   ☐ Renewal

U.S.	☐ Individual: $174	☐ Institutional: $244
Canada/Mexico	☐ Individual: $174	☐ Institutional: $304
All Others	☐ Individual: $210	☐ Institutional: $355

Call 888-378-2537 or see mailing and pricing instructions below.
Online subscriptions are available at www.interscience.wiley.com

ORDER TOTALS:

Issue / Subscription Amount: $ _____

Shipping Amount: $ _____
(for single issues only – subscription prices include shipping)

Total Amount: $ _____

SHIPPING CHARGES:

	SURFACE	DOMESTIC	CANADIAN
First Item	$5.00		$6.00
Each Add'l Item	$3.00		$1.50

(No sales tax for U.S. subscriptions. Canadian residents, add GST for subscription orders. Individual rate subscriptions must be paid by personal check or credit card. Individual rate subscriptions may not be resold as library copies.)

BILLING & SHIPPING INFORMATION:

☐ **PAYMENT ENCLOSED:** *(U.S. check or money order only. All payments must be in U.S. dollars.)*

☐ **CREDIT CARD:** ☐ VISA ☐ MC ☐ AMEX

Card number _____ Exp. Date_____

Card Holder Name_____ Card Issue # *(required)* _____

Signature _____ Day Phone_____

☐ **BILL ME:** *(U.S. institutional orders only. Purchase order required.)*

Purchase order # _____
Federal Tax ID 13559302 • GST 89102-8052

Name_____

Address_____

Phone_____ E-mail_____

Copy or detach page and send to: **John Wiley & Sons, PTSC, 5th Floor**
989 Market Street, San Francisco, CA 94103-1741

Order Form can also be faxed to: **888-481-2665**

PROMO JBXND